THE SWAN, HASTINGS
1523–1943

BY THE SAME AUTHOR

The Pubs of Hastings & St Leonards 1800–2000

Register of Licensees for Hastings & St Leonards 1500–2000

The Pubs of Rye, East Sussex 1750–1950

SECOND EDITION

THE SWAN, HASTINGS

1523–1943

David Russell

The author asserts the moral right to be identified as the author of this work. All rights reserved. No part of this publication may be reproduced, stored in a retrieval system or transmitted, in any form or by any means, electronic, mechanical, photocopying, recording or otherwise, without the prior permission of the author. This book is sold subject to the condition that it shall not, by way of trade or otherwise, be lent, resold, hired out or otherwise circulated without the author's prior consent in any form of binding or cover other than that in which it is published and without a similar condition including this condition being imposed on the subsequent purchaser.

© David Russell 2013

Published by Lynda Russell

Copies of this book are available from the publisher.
www.hastingspubhistory.com
hastings.pubs@gmail.com
Tel: 01424 200227

Printed and bound by Imprint Digital.net, Exeter

ISBN 978-0-9562917-6-9

CONTENTS

Introduction   9

CHAPTER ONE	Le Swanne	11
CHAPTER TWO	Swan as a Coaching Inn	15
CHAPTER THREE	Eighteenth Century	21
CHAPTER FOUR	The Napoleonic Wars	29
CHAPTER FIVE	Fact and Fiction	33
CHAPTER SIX	Nineteenth Century	37
CHAPTER SEVEN	Old Friendly Society	45
CHAPTER EIGHT	Swan at Play	51
CHAPTER NINE	Swan at Work	57
CHAPTER TEN	Swan Shades	63
CHAPTER ELEVEN	Joseph Collins: a Swan landlord	71
CHAPTER TWELVE	Swan Demolished & Rebuilt	77
CHAPTER THIRTEEN	From Inn to Public House	83
CHAPTER FOURTEEN	Swan in the Second World War	91
CHAPTER FIFTEEN	From Swan to Wishing Tree	97

Reference Notes   105
Bibliography   108
A Note on Sources   110

Appendix 1	Casualty list of the 1943 air raid on the Swan	111
Appendix 2	Register of Licensees	112
Appendix 3	Schedule of Tenants' Fixtures at the Swan Hotel 1886	115
Appendix 4	William Francotte paintings 1883	117

ACKNOWLEDGEMENTS

I would like to acknowledge the assistance and skills of the staff of Hastings Reference Library, Hastings Museum and Art Gallery and the East Sussex Records Office, Lewes.

The photographs on pages 60, 62, 63, 80, 82, 83, 86 (upper) and 102 are from the John Hodges archive. I am also indebted to John for the article from the Whitbreads House Journal reproduced on pages 97 and 98, and for reading an early draft of the first edition.

The photographs on pages 91 and 94 are courtesy of Nathan Goodwin. The photographs on pages 71, 74 and 76 are courtesy of Joseph and Luanne Collins. The photograph on page 89 is courtesy of Kerry Callaghan.

The photographs on pages 69, 75, 86 (lower), 90, 100, 101, 103, 104, and 120 were taken by Lynda Russell.

The watercolour of the Swan on the front cover is the work of Jean Hope, Hastings.

The drawings on pages 58, 59 and 64 are the work of James Gray. The copies of the Francombe forgeries on pages 118 and 119 are from the late Ron Fellows collection.

The theatre poster and programme on pages 52, 53 and 55 are courtesy of Hastings Museum.

I am indebted to Dr Patrick Chaplin, pub and darts historian, for reading a draft of the first edition and for contributing valuable suggestions.

Above all I would like to thank my wife Lynda for all her hard work designing, editing and publishing this book. Without her skills and dedication it would not have seen the light of day.

The house which I fix my attention upon
Is the ancient old pub we knew as the Swan.
If it's your wish a bit longer to dwell
on what has occurred at this famous hotel
Then find it here as it readily appears
Throughout an existence of 400 years.

Thomas Brandon Brett

SWAN

INTRODUCTION

My interest in the history of the Swan Inn, Hastings came about whilst researching material for *The Pubs of Hastings and St Leonards 1800–2000*, published in 2009. I was intrigued as to why the Swan, now long gone, is remembered as one of the town's most revered and respected licensed premises.

Its history has been romantically claimed as 'the history of Hastings itself', a view that has an element of truth. Why should a public house closed since 1943, evoke such veneration? The answer is twofold.

Firstly, for a relatively short but important period of its life (approximately 1770–1850), the Swan was a dispenser of luxury and prestige to royalty, gentry and wealthy visitors from the metropolitan and county elite. Secondly, many years later a totally different Swan, by then an ordinary public house, was destroyed in an air raid during the Second World War. These two aspects of its history have firmly registered the Swan in the Hastings folk memory; a memory which seems indelible and permanent.

The Swan existed for over four centuries but because the primary sources have little flesh before 1700 it is near impossible to create or reconstruct much history before that date. It is assumed therefore that sometime prior to 1700 and its time as a coaching inn, the Swan functioned as an ordinary alehouse, although little is known about its activities.

The first chapter considers its early beginnings as Le Swanne, the origins of its name and the relationship between the Swan and St Clements Church during the Reformation. This is followed by chapters on the stagecoach era, the Swan during the Napoleonic Wars and the Swan in the 18th and 19th centuries. Other chapters consider some of the artists who performed in the Swan Assembly Rooms, some Swan employees and the Old Friendly Society which had its headquarters there for over 70 years.

Chapters are included on a second licensed premises known as the Swan Shades, and on the Swan rebuilt in the late Victorian period.

SWAN

This second edition contains an additional chapter on Joseph Collins, Swan landlord from 1874 to 1884. This most welcome addition comes from the family history of Joseph Collins (2) and his wife Luanne Collins, of New York. Its inclusion is much appreciated.

This is followed by an account of the demolition and rebuilding of the Swan in 1889.

The Swan's destruction in the Second World War is the subject of the penultimate chapter and Appendix 1 lists the casualties of that tragedy. Appendix 2 is a register of licensees for both the Swan and the Shades. Appendix 3 is a tenant's fixtures list from 1886 while Appendix 4 considers the oil paintings of the Swan and the Swan Shades by William Francotte in 1883.

Oddly enough no seminal history of the Swan has been written although various local authors have reminisced on it. Journalist and local historian Thomas Brandon Brett (1816–1906) published an account in his manuscript diaries in the 1880s which he referred to as: *My History of the Swan*.[1] His account is of genealogical interest but gives no source of information.

Two other local authors Henry Cousins (1911)[2] and John Manwaring-Baines (1985)[3] both wrote briefly about the Swan in their histories of the town but left their research incomplete.

More recently an account by David Harper in his book *Whitbread: The Inn behind the Signs* (2005), claims the Swan Inn 'suffered from a witch's curse in Cromwell's day and as a consequence was burnt down and rebuilt not once but three times. And further, that after 1851 it twice burnt down again and was the location of a suicide and two serious accidents, one fatal in 1939.'[4] However, because of a lack of supporting evidence this can only be regarded as fiction. Entertaining fiction perhaps but fiction none the less. According to local author John Hodges, the source was an anonymous article entitled *The Swan, the Curse and the Wishing Tree*, published in the *Whitbread House Journal* in 1947. The article is reproduced in the final chapter as an example of the use of the public house in the creation of myth and legend.

David Russell, St Leonards-on-Sea, July 2013.

SWAN

CHAPTER ONE

LE SWANNE

Although little is known about the Swan in its early days, it survived a serious fire in the High Street during the 16th century. This fire was so devastating that most of the High Street had to be rebuilt, including five of the town's early inns and alehouses. These were the Bell, the (first) Crown, the Maidenhead, the Three Partridges and the Star—but not apparently the Swan.

The earliest known date for the Swan is 1523 when John Levet of Holyngton was the occupier of a property known as Le Swanne, on this part of the High Street.

One possible origin of the name is that it came from a local family. Swan is a Hastings family name and the Norman barons who arrived with William the Conqueror were known to have introduced many surnames into this country. The surname Swanne or Swan might well have been one of them. However, the Swan was a favoured sign in London from the early 14th century.[5]

The suffix 'Le' is also of French origin. Stephen Le Swan and Walter Le Swan for example are recorded in the Sussex Subsidy Rolls for 1296. *British History Online* points out that Le Swanne was not unknown as a pub name five centuries ago.[6] There was, for example, an alehouse called Le Swanne in Barking, Essex in 1500, and another of the same name in Holborn in 1670.

The first attempt to survey all licensed premises in England was made in 1577 when the Privy Council sent a circular letter to local magistrates 'to inquire what number of inns, taverns and alehouses are in every shire'. The reason for the survey was fiscal. Dover harbour was in bad decay and the Crown was anxious that it should be repaired. The harbour was used extensively in the war against Spain and a tax on victuallers' licences was proposed to pay for it. The local response listed 28 inns, 18 taverns and 123 alehouses within the Cinque Ports Federation. The higher cost of the Swan licence probably dated from this time.[7]

Centuries later the *Hastings and St Leonards Observer* published an anonymous article on the Swan which included several claims of doubtful validity. 'The date of its erection', it said, 'is apparently lost in the mists of antiquity, the first we learn about it being in the year 1722 when the fabric was already standing'. In that year, according to the *Observer*, 'it was known as the Swan Shades and was in the occupation of two men named Richardson and Carlton, being described as a brewery, stable yard and coach house'.[8] Thomas Brett, then writing his history of Hastings and St Leonards, borrowed some of these mistaken ideas and published them himself.

How incorrect this anonymous story was is shown by a document originally located in Hastings Museum. On 21st December 1604 one Anthony Wennell was told to 'order his inn called the Swanne in Hastings in good order and lawfull sort'! Also, in 1650 Robert Marshall, innkeeper, mortgaged his property called 'the Swanne' for £60. It seems this was only a short term loan for the deed is endorsed: 'The money on the promise is payd and the originall is cancelled'.[9]

Brett also recalled a tradition whereby certain local streets were named after the people who once lived there. He suggested that the Swan was originally known as Swan's Shades after the Swan family who, he said, are recorded living in Hastings in the 17th century and who gave their name to Swan(s) Lane or Terrace. He cites Hopper's Passage and Barley Lane as other examples of street names taken from family names.[10] However the problem with this theory is that prior to 1850 Swan Terrace was known as Church

SWAN

Street. Also the name Shades has a different origin, which is discussed later.

A century later John Manwaring-Baines remarked: 'There is a curious feature about the name'. 'John Levet died in 1534 and after the death of his son John, was succeeded by his grandson Lawrence Levett. Lawrence Levett died in 1586 and left a windmill called The Swan on the east side of Harley Shute Road, Hollington. It is an unusual name for a windmill and one wonders what significance a swan might have had for the Levet family.'[11]

The answer to this question lies in the fact that the Swan emblem has its roots in the Wars of the Roses (1455–1485). In the late Middle Ages, only 20 years before the Swan first opened its doors, livery badges were worn by both sides in the war, signifying their allegiance. Many families and private armies across the country supported the House of Lancaster. John of Gaunt, Duke of Lancaster was a major land owner in this part of the country. Because of this fact the most prevailing inn signs in East Sussex are the Swan and the White Hart, two of the armoral bearings of John O' Gaunt.

The Levet(t) family were loyal Lancastrians who showed their support for the House of Lancaster in the Wars of the Roses by adopting the symbol of a swan as a family badge, by using it as a name for their alehouse or inn in the High Street, and for their windmill in Hollington.

Another clue to the early Swan is to be found in a local legend which claims that a tunnel, now bricked up, at one time ran from the Swan to St Clements Church opposite. The tunnel is said to date back to the Reformation (1530–1650), and was apparently designed as a possible escape route for the priest in those troubled times, providing him with a direct link into the Swan!

But like all good legends, no hard evidence for the tunnel has so far come to light. Nevertheless there may be a grain of truth in this story. The business of the Reformation was to change the national religion from Catholic to Protestant, and to abolish the monasteries and any chantries (small chapels) attached to the Catholic Church.

Prior to the Reformation, the local (Catholic) church of St Clements was a centre of social activity. Neighbourhood and community activities, including plays, pageants, processions, harvest dinners, dancing, music, games and drinking (church ales, bid ales and Scot ales), were all found within the church precincts.

Under attack by the Protestant Ascendancy these activities were suppressed. In this environment alehouses and inns blossomed as they inherited and took over these former church activities. In most cases the parish church had a Church House on the boundary of its property but outside its sanctity, which took over these social functions. Further, many church houses in several areas later became licensed. The Swan and its near neighbour St Clements Church is a typical example of this post-reformation development. This should not be confused with the Church Hall in Croft Lane built in 1906.

A function of the chantry was education. We know that one, or possibly two chantries were attached to St Clements Church, and that the Swan yard later took over the original chantry garden.[12]

Also number six Swan Terrace, previously the Swan Shades, is mentioned in several deeds and documents as 'formerly the School House'. The questions must be asked: Is six Swan Terrace the site of the original chantry, and further, was the location of the Swan next door to St Clements Church a coincidence, or did the Swan perhaps start life as a Church House?

Over the years the Swan name has had several variations. After Le Swanne it was referred to simply as The Swan or in the golden age of the inn, the Swan Inn. The name 'hotel' was introduced into Britain from France sometime after 1770 but was still rare in 1800. The Swan first used the name 'hotel' in 1817. The word 'Royal' has been appended at various times, to denote royal patronage as have the words 'Family and Commercial'. Since 1523 the following names are recorded:-

1523	Le Swanne
1604–1651	The Swanne
1745–1815	Swan Inn
1817	Swan Hotel
1852	Swan and Commercial Inn
1854	Royal Swan and Commercial
1855	Swan Commercial Inn, Family Hotel and Posting House
1865–1888	Swan Hotel

SWAN

CHAPTER TWO

SWAN AS A COACHING INN

The London–Hastings Royal Mail Coach 1821, by James Pollard

The arrival of the stagecoach in the early 1700s was a major stimulus to the growth of the Swan and to the development of the (Old) town. As it took on the role of a coaching inn, the Swan became an important factor in the movement of people and goods in and out of the town and gradually expanded into the area between High Street, Hill Street and Swan Terrace.

Its early layout and design was common to coaching inns of the time with first class bedrooms and public rooms such as the 'parlors' and restaurant facing the High Street, and with other rooms along the length of Swan Terrace. The main coach entrance, later referred to as the Swan Gateway, was located on the High Street to the south of the hotel doorway. Coaches and other horse-drawn vehicles arriving at this entrance, stopped and rang for the ostler who led them into the Swan yard. An undated ground plan shows a second coach entrance from Hill Street, but this was later closed off by another stable.

From the 17th century Swan landlords acted as local postmaster for the developing Post Office, employing post boys to deliver and collect post at inns along the routes to London and elsewhere. As a posting house, the Swan provided a complete range of transport services. You could have your horse baited (fed and watered). You could hire a horse to ride or to use with your own carriage. Alternatively you could hire from a range of carriages including the post chaise, a closed fast carriage described on the Swan's bill heads as 'neat post chaise'(see page 23), or a hackney, phaeton or a 'neat gig'. In the 18th century the word 'neat' meant smart.

A cheaper mode of travel was the stagecoach, which ran between Hastings and London by the early 1700s. Stagecoaches were cumbersome and heavy vehicles, often without springs, which combined with poor road conditions provided a rough and uncomfortable journey. Prosperous first class passengers rode inside, second class passengers sat in an open 'basket' attached to the back of the vehicle, while third class passengers sat on the roof with the luggage, holding on to a handrail.

By mid-century the Swan had acquired several coach houses, stables with granaries, a harness room and a brew house. But it still had two gardens within its boundaries.

By now the average coach speed had increased to 10 miles per hour, but there was still only one return journey a week between Hastings and London. A card issued by the proprietors of the Regulator or White Coach in 1745 stated: 'This fast coach will leave the Swan Inn, Hastings, at four o'clock on Monday mornings arriving at Robertsbridge the same day, Sevenoaks the next and London the third, returning to Hastings the three following days.'[13] The Regulator was a four horse coach, a 'four in hand' driven by a Mr Charles Paul, otherwise known as Old Charlie. It seems that drivers and guards were poorly paid but made a good living from tips, for looking after luggage, post and valuables.

In 1784 the Post Office introduced Royal Mail coaches which had right of way on the road, with a guard announcing arrivals and departures on the post horn. He also carried a blunderbuss and two

BOLT-IN-TUN

ROYAL MAIL & COACH ESTABLISHMENT,

Sussex Tavern and Family Hotel,

FLEET STREET, LONDON.

Royal Mails.

PORTSMOUTH & ISLE of WIGHT, With a Branch to Chichester, Bognor, & Petworth.

HASTINGS & TUNBRIDGE WELLS, With a Branch to Rye and Hawkhurst.

Every Evening .... at Half-past Seven o'Clock.

Fast Coaches.

	Morning	Afternoon
ABERYSTWITH, Kington, Penybont, and Rhayader	7	4
ALRESFORD, Alton, and Farnham	8	
BATH, Melksham, Devizes, Marlborough, and Hungerford	7	¼ to 7
BIRMINGHAM, Stratford-on-Avon, Shipston, and Woodstock	7	
BLACKWATER, Sandhurst (Royal Military College,) Egham, and Staines		3
BRISTOL, Clifton, Bath, Devizes, and Newbury	7	¼ to 7
BRIGHTON, Reigate, and Crawley	½ past 8 ½ past 10	
CHELTENHAM, Witney, and Oxford	7 & ¼ to 8	½ past 4
CHICHESTER, Midhurst, Haslemere, Petworth, and Godalming	9	½ past 7
CHERTSEY, Shepperton, Halliford, Sunbury, and Hampton	½ past 8	½ past 4
CAERMARTHEN, Llandilo, Llandovery, Brecon, and Crickowell	7	4
DOVER, Deal, Canterbury, Sittingbourne, and Rochester	9	½ past 6
ESHER, Claremont, Ditton, and Kingston	8 & 9	½ past 3
EXETER, Collumpton, Wellington, Bridgewater, Taunton, and Wells	7	¼ to 7
FROME, Trowbridge, and Devizes	7	
GLOUCESTER, Cheltenham, Northleach, Burford, Witney, and Oxford *(In direct communication with Coaches for all parts of South Wales.)*	7 & ¼ to 8	½ past 4
GODALMING, Guildford, Ripley, Cobham, and Esher	8 & 9	¼ to 3
HAMPTON COURT, Hampton, Twickenham, and Richmond	8 & ½ p. 10	½ past 3 ½ past 6

	Morning	Afternoon
HEREFORD, Ross, Gloucester, Cheltenham, and Oxford	¼ to 7	½ past 4
HASTINGS, Battle, Robertsbridge, Flimwell, and Tunbridge	10	½ past 7
MARGATE and Ramsgate	9	½ past 6
MONMOUTH, Whitchurch, and Ross	7	4
OXFORD	7 & 8	4
PORTSMOUTH, Horndean, Petersfield, Liphook, and Godalming	½ past 8	2 ½ past 7
READING, Wokingham, Bracknell, and Virginia Water	½ past 11	4
RYE, Northiam, Sandhurst, Hawkhurst, and Lamberhurst	11	½ past 7
SHREWSBURY, Bridgenorth, and Kidderminster	7	4
SOUTHAMPTON, Winchester, Alton, Farnham, and Guildford	½ past 8	
St. LEONARDS and Hastings	10	½ past 7
SEVEN OAKS and Riverhead	10 & 11	½ past 3
SWANSEA, Neath, Cowbridge, Cardiff, Newport, and Chepstow	7	4
TUNBRIDGE WELLS, Tunbridge, and Seven Oaks	10	½ past 2 ½ past 7
WARMINSTER, Trowbridge, and Devizes	7	
WEYBRIDGE, Oatlands, Walton, Moulsey, and Hampton Court		½ past 3
WINCHESTER and Farnham	8	
WINDSOR, Eton, and Slough (Patronized by Her Majesty.)	½ past 8 ½ past 9	½ past 2 4
WORCESTER and Tewkesbury	7	4
WALLINGFORD and Henley	8	

ROBERT GRAY & CO. Proprietors.

Every information relative to the different **STEAM PACKETS** from

BRISTOL .... to Cork, Waterford, Swansea, Ilfracomb, Haverfordwest, and Tenby.
PORTSMOUTH .... to the Isle of Wight, Torquay, Plymouth, and Falmouth.
SOUTHAMPTON .... to the Isle of Wight, Guernsey, Jersey, St. Maloes, Havre de Grace, France, and Italy.

☞ **NOTICE.**—No Parcel, or Passenger's Luggage, will be accounted for above the Value of **Ten Pounds** unless entered as such, and Insurance paid accordingly.

pistols. The London–Hastings Royal Mail coaches began about 10 years later and these were the fastest and most expensive mode of transport to date. These coaches were originally designed for a driver and up to four inside passengers. The guard travelled on the outside at the rear next to the mail box.

By 1797 the three day journey to London had been reduced to one day, changing at Tonbridge. A local guide book stated: 'A Stage coach runs between London and Hastings every Monday, Thursday and Saturday throughout the year; and on Wednesday also, during the summer season:- it sets out from the Swan Inn, Hastings at five, and from the Bolt In Tun Inn, Fleet Street, London at six in the morning; the two coaches meet at Tonbridge about noon, where they exchange passengers and parcels and return home at night.'[14]

The 1817 *Hastings Guide* stated: 'Convenient and expeditious Coaches run to and from London daily, from the Swan, the Crown, and the Castle Hotels. A coach also goes daily to Brighton during the summer and three times a week in the winter; alternately passing through Lewes and Eastbourne: another Coach also leaves twice a week for Rye, Romney, Hithe, Folkstone, Dover and Margate.'[15]

A painting by James Pollard in 1821 shows the London–Hastings Royal Mail coach being pulled by two bay and two piebald horses. This service was expanded six years later in 1827 when the *Sussex Weekly Advertiser* could boast that the 'mail coaches it must be confessed, add respectability to the town to which they are attached … we have pleasure in communicating … so desirable an acquisition of two Royal Mail coaches … to run to and from the metropolis daily, one leaving Hastings every evening at nine o'clock and the other returning from London to Hastings every morning at a little before five.'[16]

But there was always an element of danger. In 1801 the London–Hastings Mail coach was stopped and robbed of its mail bags by two men near Farnborough. In the same year the mail bags on the Hastings–Rye Royal Mail coach were carried off in a similar manner. James, John and Sarah Austin were arrested for the robbery and notes to the value of £82, belonging to the Hastings Bank, were recovered. The robbers were tried in London.

SWAN

In 1822 the London–Hastings coach heading for the Swan, overturned in Whatlington and went down a bank with a broken axle. An inside lady passenger injured her back and other passengers were bruised. In 1836 there was another serious accident in Ore, when the coach overturned in a severe snow storm injuring the horses. It took 20 men to dig the coach out of the snow. The injured horses were replaced and taken to the Swan 'Ostry', a special stable for the treatment and recuperation of sick horses.

A report in 1848 recorded the arrival of the London–Hastings coach. The post horn had now been replaced by the key-bugle. 'The clear notes of a key-bugle were borne to my ears; *The Light of Other Days* correctly and tastefully played, came swelling and dying through the street. I distinguished the cheerful trampling of horses accompanying the music and saw a well loaded coach coming quickly along finishing its journey in triumphant style.' The writer expressed a certain nostalgia for the stage coach, 'there was something lifelike, nay human, about the whole affair. As it passed by me I read the word Hastings painted on the side of the vehicle.'[17]

From the beginning of the 19th century the key-bugle was played not only on the coaches but also in light opera and in military bands. To be a coach guard was the aim of many ex-army bandsmen.

But the writing was on the wall for Hastings coaching days. With the opening of Hastings railway station in 1851 the stagecoach and the Royal Mail coach saw their final days. The role of the coaching inns in the movement of people gradually faded as the railways took over. Swan landlord, William Carswell, was reduced to delivering and collecting the mail from the railway station. He advertised 'Royal Mail Omnibuses from the Swan Hotel to and from every train'.

Carriers however, on market days in particular, continued delivering goods from the Swan yard for the rest of the century. Battle, Brede, Fairlight, Pevensey, Robertsbridge and Winchelsea were all serviced from here.

There was much nostalgia with the passing of the stage coach just as future generations would mourn the steam train and later still the vintage car.

SWAN

LONDON COACHES

FARES REDUCED!

THE REGULATOR & PARAGON,

FOUR Inside'Light Post Coaches, from the Swan and Castle Hotels, Hastings, every Morning at a quarter before Nine o'clock, to the White Horse Cellar, Piccadilly, Bolt-in-Tun, Fleet-street, and Belle Sauvage, Ludgate-hill.

    Fares Inside   .   .   .   12s.
    Ditto Outside   .   .   .   8s.

A considerable Reduction in the Carriage of Parcels.

Advert 1830

THE ROAD ONCE MORE.—When we at the close of last Autumn informed our readers that the last coach on the road to London from this town had ceased to run, we lamented over the fact as an event to be deplored by all the lovers of a delightful coach ride, such as is to be perceived by every one journeying from London to Hastings—a ride, which for beauty of scenery and diversity of view, is not to be equalled by any sixty miles out of London. In that paragraph we consigned, then and for ever, the road coach to the tomb of its fathers, believing it to be in future spoken of as a thing that had been. We are, however, delighted, as will numbers of your readers, to find that by the spirited and determined exertions of one individual alone, a coach is again on the road, journeying from Hastings to London. Mr. J. Watson, so well known on this road, has become the sole proprietor of a well appointed coach which started on Monday. We believe that he starts with the good wishes of the town, and of those on the road for his success, and that and a little exertion on each individual's part, will tend to secure it. We certainly think the inhabitants of this town owe it to themselves to use an effort to continue a coach, for without it all communication with the line of old road upwards is cut off, as it has been for the last six months, to the detriment of the town.

Sussex Express 15.04.1848

SWAN

CHAPTER THREE

EIGHTEENTH CENTURY

John Collier, owner of the Swan
1758–1760

In 1727 Hastings Corporation was presented with a vast, solid silver punch bowl by the Hastings Barons (Cinque Ports officials) who had attended the coronation of George II. The punch bowl, which was used at civic functions in the Swan and elsewhere, weighed 164 ounces [1.2 kilos] and held 17 quarts [19.32 litres] of punch, a mixture of spirits and hot water (or milk), sugar, lemon and spices.

One of the Barons was John Collier, whose wealthy family owned the Swan from about 1758 to 1771. On his death in 1760 ownership passed to his widow Mary, and on her death in 1766 to their daughter Henrietta 'who had paid for repairs to the Swan then the testator's property'.[18] Ownership then passed to her brother-in-law General James Murray.

Another daughter, also Mary, in a letter to her mother in 1749 wrote: 'We were at ye Swan yesterday to keep ye Birthday, but can't say there was a very Brilliant Sett of Company. Tho' we had a Ball, and Mr

Silver Punch Bowl

Polhill and Mr Bayley were some of ye Head of ye Dancers. I Danc'd with little George Coulton, who was as well as any Body.'[19]

A noted landlord was Thomas Hovenden (1771–1775) who continued supplying the needs of wealthy visitors. In 1772 he enlarged the Swan when he opened the new Assembly Room on the first floor looking out over the High Street. This very large neo-classical style room, was adorned with seven figurines of the Greek Muses each five

SWAN

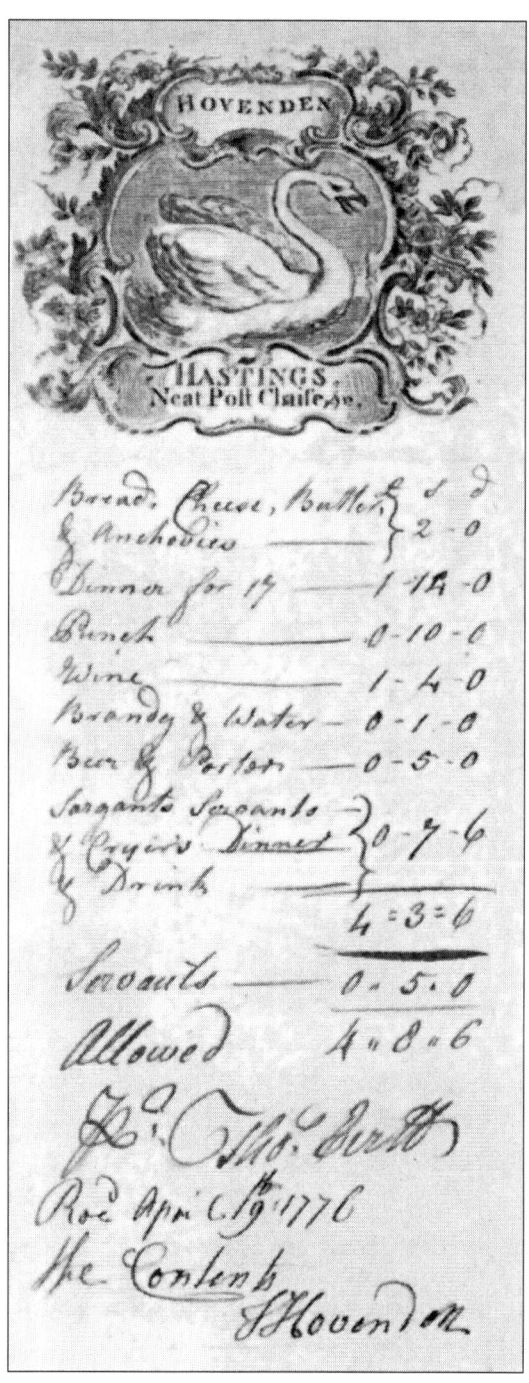

Bill for dinner and drinks 1776

feet high and each holding a branch of candles, later gasoliers. Some years later it was described as having a music gallery, which was probably a reference to a raised podium on two deal platforms underneath an arch at one end of the room. But its main features were the 10 feet [3.05m] wide handsome marble fire place and the 12 feet [3.66m] bay window overlooking the High Street. A ground plan of the Swan in 1836 shows one entrance to the Assembly Room on the south side of the High Street adjoining a shop, later a hairdressers. The main entrance to the Assembly Room, however, was via a wide staircase in the hotel lobby.

Thomas Hovenden

A plan of the Assembly Room a century later in 1880 gives its size as 53 feet x 24 feet [16.1m x 7.3m]. A pencilled note referring to the furniture says: 'Note:- Tables are 42 feet [12.8m] long as set up.'

Thomas Hovenden proudly advertised his new acquisition in the *Sussex Weekly Advertiser*:- 'A very Neat and Commodious Ball and Assembly Room is nearly Finished, for the Convenience of such as wish to amuse themselves in that Way.'[20]

The Swan Assembly Room opened to the public in the summer of 1772. It was apparently such an immediate success that Thomas Hovenden issued a second notice advertising weekly 'Card Assemblies' every Monday where the popular 18th century card games of Euchre and Pharaoh were played. 'All Gentlemen and Ladies to pay 1s.6d. for Tea, Coffee and Cards, at coming in. It is intended that once at least in every Month there will be a Ball, viz. on the Monday nearest the Full Moon; all Dancers to pay One Shilling towards the expense of the Musick; and likewise to pay for Negus, Wines, etc. which they order to be brought into the Ball Room. N.B. No Supper will be provided unless ordered.'[21]

Negus was a popular 18th century beverage for the fashionable classes. It was essentially a hot port and lemon sweetened with sugar and spiced with nutmeg. It took its name from Colonel Francis Negus, its creator.

In 1775 Thomas Hovenden gave up the Swan to become proprietor of the Starr on the opposite side of the High Street, where he was to remain for the next 20 years. The Starr became the Roebuck Inn in 1840.

Thomas Hovenden was followed as landlord by William Scrivens, a joint-proprietor of the Hastings Circulating Library, one of the first libraries to open in the town in 1788. It had a large stock of books as well as children's literature and newspapers, and organised musical evenings. He was also a proprietor of the increasingly popular 'machines for bathing' then coming into vogue in resorts such as Bognor, Brighton and Margate.

SEA BATHING

Mr. and Mrs. SCRIVENS respectfully inform the Nobility and Gentry, &c. that intend visiting Hastings this season, for Bathing (where every necessary Convenience for that Purpose is provided,) that they have fitted up a large and convenient House, for the Reception of those that wish to be accommodated with Board and Lodging, where every Attention will be paid to render it agreeable to those that are pleased to favour them with their Company.
N.B. A COACH four Times a Week, to the BOLT-IN-TUN, Fleet-Street, London.

Sussex Weekly Advertiser 25.6.1787

In the 1780s before the existence of a local police force, Hastings experienced a rise in serious criminal activity and groups of inhabitants organised themselves for protection. One such society was formed at the Swan:- 'to raise a fund to prosecute offenders who shall be found guilty of robbing or defrauding any members of the said Society of their property. We, the Society give notice that we will pay several REWARDS ... for the conviction of any person stealing Fence, Wood, Coals, Garden Stuff, Fruit, Fowls or such (two Guineas) and any person wilfully murdering any member of the Society (ten Guineas) etc. The days of meeting of this Society are the first Thursday in March and September between Six and Seven in the evening.'

SWAN

Incredibly, two audacious highway robbers using the aliases of William Johnson Esquire and Samuel Watson Esquire and posing as 'gentlemen who moved in polite circles', patronised the Swan lounge at the same time as the above society. They lived in a rented mansion in Winchelsea where they provided elegant entertainments and kept servants in livery. Among their vehicles were a chariot and a phaeton drawn by horses, admired for their breed and capabilities and well known to the ostlers in the Swan yard.

But their lifestyle was funded by robbing the mail coaches, until one day a passenger on the Bristol coach, someone who in fact they had dined with in the Swan, recognised them. They were pursued, captured and imprisoned but after escaping, then re-caught and tried, were finally executed at Tyburn. The above Society continued meeting at the Swan!

Nature was another threat. Abnormal weather conditions had a profound effect on the town and the Swan in the year 1785, and again in 1792. On both occasions there was a combination of an abnormally high tide and a high wind, compelling local fishermen to haul their boats up the High Street as far as the Swan Gateway for safety. The shoreline was then much further in than today.

On both occasions the inundation to which the lower part of the town was subjected, blocked off the High Street for several days and coaches had to be parked some distance from the inn.

Throughout the 18th century the development of old Hastings was financed by privateering and smuggling. At that time there were frequent conflicts between the English and French in the Channel. Many English vessels, known as privateers, were commissioned by the government as 'men of war' to cruise against French, Spanish and rebel colonial (American) ships and to take any goods, wares and merchandise from them. In other words they had government permission to engage in piracy on the high seas. They were also used for smuggling.

The following report – one of many – appeared in 1759:

On Tuesday last a Barley Vessel bound for this Town was attacked by a French Privateer between Bexhill and Hastings; but after an Engagement of two Hours she obliged Monsieur to sheer off, though she mounted but six Guns and had but four

SWAN

Men and a Boy on board and the Privateer 10 four Pounders and full of Men; the Brig was greatly shattered and damaged.[22]

Fast-sailing cutters built locally in the yards of Ransome and Ridley, and Winter and Thwaites, were sold in the Swan sale room before being launched from the beach. Second-hand boats were also sold.

> *To be sold to the best Bidder,*
> At the Swan, at Hasting, on Friday, the 16th of this Instant March,
> THE LYON Cutter Privateer, John Grayling, Commander, now lying in Rye Harbour, being a most excellent prime Sailer, Burthen about eighty Tons, mounting ten Carriage Guns, four Four Pounders, and six Three-Pounders, besides Swivels, with two complete Setts of Sails, extremely well fitted and sound, the best of Accommodations for sixty Men, ready for Sea at a Day's Notice, and only one Year old. Inventories to be delivered at the Place of Sale.
> Enquire for further Particulars of Mr. Thomas Breed, at the Swan, at Hasting.

Sussex Weekly Advertiser 5.3.1759

> *To be sold to the best Bidder,*
> At the Swan, at Hasting, on Friday, the 16th of this Instant March,
> THE FOX Cutter Privateer, Richard Harman, Commander, now lying on Hasting Beach, being a most remarkable good Sailer, Burthen about seventy Tons, mounting eight Carriage Guns, Four and Three Pounders, besides Swivels with almost two complete Setts of Sails, extremely well fitted and sound, very good Accommodations for forty Men, ready for sea immediately, and only one Year old. Inventories to be delivered at the Place of Sale.
> Enquire for Particulars of Mr. Thomas Breed, at the Swan, at Hasting.

Sussex Weekly Advertiser 5.3.1759

SWAN

In the final years of the 18th century and into the next century, it was the custom on the completion of a new boat to open the shipyard to the public. Visitors to the Swan took advantage.

> The Yard of Messrs. Winter and Thwaites was this day opened for the free admission of the public to inspect a new Merchant brig, *(The Mark Breeds)* upwards of 150 tons, elegantly modelled, and built by the above gentlemen. A great number of ladies and gentlemen availed themselves of the opportunity thus afforded, by going on board the vessel, and were much gratified with the excellence of her construction, and the polite attention of the proprietor. An accommodating ladder was placed at the eastern side of the brig, defended by sails, enabling the ladies to ascend without difficulty; the yards were manned by sailors dressed in white frocks and trowsers, the sails were unfurled, and flags were displayed on the foremast, mainmast, and peak-end. The Arcade Parade, and shingles were lined with spectators, the *toute ensemble* producing an animated and pleasing effect, — "Success to the Mark Breeds" was drank amidst the reiterated huzzas of the assemblage.[23]

According to Brett, it was the custom at this time for local merchants and shipbuilders to give dinners before final settlement of the year's accounts. These 'Settling Dinners' were held at the Swan and other public houses. It was also the custom to hold the annual Pierwarden's dinner at the Swan. The pierwarden was officially responsible for enforcing local bye-laws relating to Hastings beach.

These were prosperous times for Hastings, and the Assembly Room was kept busy as an auction house disposing of boats, land and property:-

> March 1st, 1790. To be sold at the house of William Scrivens, the Swan Inn, Hastings.
> (Lot 1), 74 acres of pasture land on Pevensey Marsh, occupied by Abraham Langham.
> (Lot 2), Knockbridge Farm at Icklesham and Fairlight, occupied by Thomas Cooper.
> (Lot 3), Pannell Wood, adjoining Lot 2 at Fairlight. About 14 acres.
> Apply Mr Ade, Auctioneer, Battle.

Sussex Weekly Advertiser 1.3.1790

SWAN

CHAPTER FOUR

THE NAPOLEONIC WARS

In the build-up to the Napoleonic Wars (1796–1815) skirmishes between English and French vessels in the English Channel were a regular occurrence. The press reported in 1781 that: 'three small British vessels, one armed, gave battle to two armed French frigates. Two days later the same French frigates seized a British brig off Brighton. The British made reprisals by capturing one of the frigates and her 20 guns. The French ship was surrounded by four cutters and a sturdy brig. As the fleet passed Hastings with its prize the people on shore were visibly moved with excitement, and revelled in lusty cheers when they saw the tri-colour hauled down and the Union Jack run up in its place.'[24]

At that time a good view of the sea could be had from the Swan.

A French Cutter

SWAN

In the 1790s several meetings were announced by the Town Crier, expressing concerns about the large influx of soldiers shortly to be billeted in Hastings:- 'Whereas at the last meeting of the inhabitants of this town at the Swan Inn it was resolved that in case an extraordinary number of soldiers should be quartered here, a General Meeting of the town should be called and as it is understood a very large number of soldiers are coming here today. The inhabitants are particularly requested to meet at the Swan at half past nine o'clock this morning to take the same into consideration.'

The military did indeed arrive in 'extraordinary number' and many were billeted in the town's public houses and inns. The Cavalry militia took over most of the extensive Swan stables and granaries, officers were billeted in the Swan, and other ranks in the Swan Tap. Large numbers were also billeted at Fairlight, Halton, Bopeep and elsewhere.

In September 1794, landlord William Scrivens was commissioned by officers from Fairlight to decorate the Assembly Room and the stairs, to 'depict the pomp and pomposity of glorious war' for a series of balls. It was reported that 'all the rank and fashion of Hastings attended these balls and two hundred ladies and gentlemen from within six miles radius were present'.

Because of the threat of an invasion by Napoleon, the town voted a £100 donation to government defence costs. To meet the cost of this donation, reductions were made in corporation expenditure including the cost of public dinners at the Swan. Instructions were also given that 'At election of Mayor and other public dinners ... servants who wait at table should be allowed a certain sum each in lieu of drinks, to prevent imposition below stairs, say half a crown each and dinner'. Usually, half the cost of such dinners, a large amount, went on beer, brandy and punch.

In August 1797 the booming cannons were distinctly heard from the beach during a bombardment of the French coast, and reports were received of Nelson's victory over the French fleet near Rosetta.

In October 1801 the bells of St Clements were rung when the welcome news that a peace treaty had been agreed between England and France, reached Hastings. There was much celebration in the Swan and in other public houses, but the peace was short lived and by 1803 war had broken out again.

SWAN

British Infantry 1800

Two years later news was received of Nelson's victory over the combined French and Spanish fleets at Trafalgar, and the Swan hosted another celebration. An artist was engaged to paint a scene of the battle, and the picture was hung in the Assembly Room.

In 1806 Sir Arthur Wellesley (later the Duke of Wellington) arrived in Hastings to take charge of a brigade of militia waiting for the expected invasion, and the Swan hosted yet another celebration.

There is a certain irony in the fact that all these dinners and celebrations were held at the Swan during the Napoleonic Wars, when in 1809 three escaping French prisoners of war, who seemed to have plenty of money and a very good command of English, booked into the Swan incognito.

One night when all had retired and Hastings and the Swan were fast asleep, the three men slid down a rope of bedclothes from their room above the Swan yard in an attempt to flee the country. They were promptly confronted by the pub dog and the resulting commotion aroused the neighbourhood. The Swan's three unusual 'guests' retreated undetected back into their room, and even complained to the landlord for allowing such a din preventing honest men from sleeping!

The following night they tried again. This time they managed to reach the Stade where they commandeered a small boat, but were challenged and attacked by a fisherman seeking a reward. They were charged with leaving the Swan without paying, but the cruel wounds they had received at the hands of the fisherman found some sympathy in the court.

Landlord Thomas Stockwell was also sympathetic and told the court of their good behaviour in his house, and that they had left money for him far in excess of what they owed. Finally the charge was dismissed but they were still found guilty of escape and sent to a prison hulk moored on the River Medway. An area known as Grange near the Medway was at that time 'within the Liberties of Hastings' and under its jurisdiction as a Cinque Port.

But on arrival in Chatham their luck began to change and their third attempt at escape was a success when, in a stolen rowing boat, they finally managed to reach Boulogne.

SWAN

CHAPTER FIVE

FACT AND FICTION

The account of French prisoners of war at the Swan was recorded by William Branch-Johnson in his book *Wolves of the Channel*, published in 1931.[25]

Many years before, another author, John Byng, recorded in a travel diary his journeys through England, including a visit to Hastings and the Swan in 1788. On the way from Rye with his travel companion Isaac Dalby, a noted mathematician, he described the descent into Hastings as:

> ... very pleasant: but the town is narrow streeted, and ill paved. At the farther end of the main street, and near the sea, is the Swan, the principal inn, where we order'd for our dinner the old fare, for no fish is to be had; of which I had hoped much at Winchelsea, and more here; but there is always some excuse of wind, or idleness, to prevent the fishermen.
>
> This town stands between two hills, and immediately upon the sea; but it is a bad shore for bathing, tho there is allways

John Byng   Isaac Dalby

a summer company there. After walking the beach, we ascended the steep hill to the right, on whose summit are the poor remains of the castle, built by Willm the Conqueror.

We searched many turf-traps set for wheat-ears, when the custom is to leave a penny for every caught bird you take away. Within the castle, we seated ourselves for some time, delighted with the weather, the freshness of the sea-breeze and the cheerfulness of the scenery; till the shepherd came to survey his traps, when we paid him seven pence for his capture of seven birds, whom we sat instantly to pluck in preparation of our dinner spit; and it wou'd have made others laugh to have seen us at our poulterers work; which, being finsh'd, we hasten'd back to the inn, but were delay'd by going into a circulating-library, where I.D. recognised in the master an old ship-mate.

We had for dinner a roasted duck, cold beef, and plumb pye, with 3 wheatears and an half each; 5 that came to us afterwards were left behind.[26]

In the 1830s another author, Theodore Hook, described a visit to the Swan in his novel *Jack Brag*, where Jack spent an evening in the company of an eccentric colonial who had just arrived in Hastings from India.[27] The period is just before landlord William Eldridge became bankrupt. Wheatears are not mentioned this time but raspberry tartlet is!

The following is paraphrased from the novel:
'It was lateish in the evening when he (Jack Brag) reached Hastings, and was driven to that admirable inn, The Swan, which combines all the attributes which a man does not require in a house of that sort. Jack bundled out of his yellow-and-two,' [a Phaeton drawn by two horses], and wanting to socialise went into the 'ill-smelling coffee-room, and contented himself with ordering a bed, a glass of hot brandy and water' and a sandwich which he described as 'dirt, butter and mustard, laid between two bits of stale bread'.

Jack sat looking at the drink which had been placed before him while waiting for his servant. At nine o'clock a scuffling noise outside the coffee-room door aroused his attention. Turning his eyes to the source of the disturbance, he beheld a slim, pale, and what he called an 'interesting-looking' man, enter the room 'some what feebly, assiduously wrapped up in divers and sundry coats and cloaks; his face peeping out from under a fanciful kind of foraging cap, overlaid by a pink silk handkerchief'.

The man sat down in a state of exhaustion and told the waiter to tip the hotel porter 'and tell Rummagee-Doss to bring me some eau de Cologne'. The waiter disappeared. 'I beg your pardon, sir', said the stranger to Brag, 'but I am a sad invalid, so low and miserable from ill health, that I prefer this corner of the coffee-room to any private room of my own and, I am afraid, I cause a great deal of inconvenience I declare'.

'I have just arrived from India', said the stranger, who later introduced himself as Narcissus Fripps. He began to complain about his journey. 'I never suffered anything like the wretchedness of the voyage: such a set of people, no sentiment, no delicacy about them, so rough and noisy, and I so extremely indisposed, the moment I could, I got on shore here. I brought nothing but half a dozen packages of things I wanted, and my man, Rummagee-Doss, just to take care of me a little.'

Theodore Hook

SWAN

'If you are not going to turn in just yet', said Jack, 'I'll order another glass of "hot" to keep you company.' At this point Rummagee-Doss, the Indian servant, arrived: 'a fine-looking piece of brown humanity, done up in muslin, with a high-caste yellow streak down his forehead, bearing a bottle of eau de Cologne'. 'That's a rummish cut of a toggery', said Jack, who had never seen an Indian servant before. 'A what?' said the stranger. 'Curious dress', said Jack.

'I am going to have a little weak tea', said the stranger, 'and a raspberry tart, I think I shall indulge myself for I am very unwell'. 'Tea and tarts', said Jack, 'that's what I call a queer cross; but I suppose you chaps from the East have a great many varieties of feed of which we know nothing'.

At this point in the conversation the waiter arrived with a tray on which 'a tea equippage was arranged and sure enough three raspberry tartlets, ovals of jam covered with a treillage of pastry'. Jack looked at the tarts, wondered about the taste of his new companion, and ordered another glass of brandy.

Jack Brag is, of course, a novel and cannot be assumed as fact. However, it is interesting to speculate that Rumagee-Doss was an early ethnic immigrant to visit Hastings!

At this time in the 1820s and 1830s many ships on international voyages moored off shore at Hastings on their way to London Docks, and some of their passengers were brought ashore by the ferry man. Passengers who had spent, in some cases, months at sea, were glad to disembark at Hastings and after a period of rest, continue their journey to London by coach. Inns such as the Swan and the Anchor in George Street were only too pleased to get the custom.

In 1838 for example, it was reported, 'Arrived off Hastings on Monday the ship "William Nichol", Captain John McAlpine from Sydney to London, 106 days landed at Daniel's Anchor Inn J. Bettington Esq and Mr Hillditch,' and other passengers 'for the Swan'.

> A lugger landed 20 persons here, who were passengers from Melbourne by a passing vessel the 'Monarch' which had been four months on the voyage. The vessel also brought gold to the value of £171,000.

Sussex Express 25.06.1859

SWAN

CHAPTER SIX

NINETEENTH CENTURY

Between 1814 and 1817 the (Old) town doubled in size and the influx of fashionable visitors increased. The Swan, and the Crown (which finally closed in 2012), were described as 'the principle rendezvous of gentility', and Hastings itself became one of the most fashionable seaside resorts in the country, a trend which unfortunately was over by the 1840s.

This trend led to uncontrolled and unplanned development of the town with the building of many small houses mainly in the gardens of bigger and older properties. This in turn led to overcrowding, and by the mid 1830s, to the creation of slum property and poverty.

The Swan Assembly Room was by this time a widely used social venue. It was at various times used as a market, a theatre, a sale room, an election headquarters, an auction house, a lecture room for the Mechanics Institute, a ballroom and a venue for the Hastings Flower Show. In 1784 the Assembly Room was even used to interview potential pupils for Hastings Grammar School.

In 1823 the Old Town Hall, a few doors away from the Swan, was rebuilt and the Quarter Sessions were for a time transferred to the Swan. One case brought up was that of a man who, on being found guilty, received seven years transportation to Australia for stealing some rolls of cloth and a pair of boots in All Saints Street.

The Assembly Room was also the location for most of the town's important municipal and civic functions and for some of the formalities of the Cinque Ports Federation.

The end of the 18th century and the French Revolution influenced a swelling of public interest in the franchise and the right to vote, and feelings were running high. Hastings had two Members of Parliament at this time but, although by 1830 the population of the town had increased to 10,000, only 30 people had the vote, which they mostly paid for by 'Scot and Lotte', a form of municipal tax allowing the payer to vote in parliamentary elections. Neither of the Hastings members of parliament supported reform.

SWAN

But in January 1831 the Swan presented a festive scene. The bells of St Clements were rung when 130 people attended an Independent Reform Dinner. Reformers were much excited by the prospect of a Reform Bill becoming law, and ratepayers who paid rates of £10 or more becoming eligible to vote.

Speakers at a series of Swan meetings called upon Hastings to 'wrest its liberty from the grasp of the borough mongers who were fanning the dying embers of corruption'. A petition in favour of reform was prepared, and in one day 'whilst lying at the Swan' it received over 600 signatures. This (national) campaign finally culminated in the passing of the Great Reform Bill of 1832 on the 'Glorious First of June'.

A noted celebration at the Swan was in 1850 when £300 was raised by public subscription to fund a dinner to celebrate Hastings banker Thomas Farncombe becoming Lord Mayor of London. The event was attended by men only. The drawing below hung in the hotel lobby for many years afterwards.[28] On civic occasions such as these the most popular drink was punch served from the Corporation Punch Bowl. However, by the 1840s punch had gone

Celebration for the Lord Mayor of London 1850

THE HASTINGS & ST. LEONARDS NEWS.

HASTINGS, FRIDAY, APRIL 5, 1850.

THE GRAND BANQUET.

WE understand that every preparation is being made, for the reception of the LORD MAYOR OF LONDON in this borough on Wednesday next in a manner becoming his station.

The dinner is to be served precisely at six o'clock, and it is the desire of the committee that every guest will present himself at the Swan Hotel before that hour. Everyone present at the banquet is to appear in uniform or full dress. Among the company there will be the EARL OF CHICHESTER, Earl WALDEGRAVE, Viscount CHEWTON, and several of the City dignitaries. The "loving cup" is to go round on the occasion. The Hastings band is to attend, as well as several professional singers from London, the latter being engaged through Mr. ACRAMAN. A toast-master will also come from London.

The whole of the arrangements are to be carried out in the most munificent style, and we doubt not that the scene will be a brilliant one. It shall be our object, in our impression of the following Friday, to present our readers with an ample report of the proceedings and addresses. His lordship is expected to arrive on Wednesday, accompanied by his chaplain, secretary, and officers.

out of fashion, and in 1850 it was reported that: 'punch is now disused, and has long ceased to be a fashionable liquor, and the Corporation preferring wine at their public festivals, a framework of wood has been made to fit inside the bowl, to hold decanters: by this means it still forms a handsome appendage at their dinners, and constitutes a grand centre ornament to the table.'

Another addition to the décor of the Inn was a stuffed swan which had been shot by landlord George Robinson in 1840. This poor creature was part of a wedge of swans flying over the town in formation and as a fixture in the Bar Parlour was the nearest the Swan had to an inn sign.

In 1854 another celebration was held for Hastings resident, Captain Robert McClure. In 1848 McClure made an arduous and distant voyage to the Canadian Arctic in search of a missing explorer, John Franklin.

Franklin had been searching for the Northwest Passage, a navigable channel that was believed to connect the North Atlantic and Pacific oceans. His search was a long chapter of failure, disaster and tragedy, but also of heroism and endurance. Franklin and his crew disappeared in 1845 and several expeditions went out to rescue them. In the dreadful winter of 1847 Franklin's two ships became icebound and their crews perished. Franklin is remembered as the 'man who ate his own boots'.

Captain Robert McClure

In his ship, Investigator, McClure was the final explorer to look for Franklin. In so doing he discovered the fabled Northwest Passage himself, also became icebound and eventually had to abandon ship. After two years living on the ice McClure and his crew, which included several Hastings men, were rescued by the navy and the Investigator was abandoned to the ice floes.

On their return home McClure was knighted and awarded £5,000 by the government. His crew were awarded a further £5,000 between them. The celebration menu at the Swan was:

1st course: Turbot, cod, mock turtle and oxtail soup.
2nd course: Turkey, geese, curried fowl, roast and stewed beef, lamb, mutton, ham and tongues.
3rd course: Game, pheasant, partridge, duck and hare.
4th course: Plums, jellies, creams and custards.[29]

SWAN COMMERCIAL INN,
Family Hotel, and Posting House,
HIGH STREET, HASTINGS,
SUSSEX.

The Proprietor, WILLIAM CARSWELL, in respectfully soliciting the patronage of the Nobility, Gentry, and Commercial World, begs leave to intimate to them that at this well-known Establishment, which is the oldest established Hotel, may be found comfort, elegance, and retirement, comprising as it does, superior suites of well-arranged commodious Apartments.

The limits of an advertisement are too circumscribed to admit of fully expatiating on the beauties and attractions of this far-famed Watering Place, yet W. C. trusts he may not be deemed arrogant by those who have honoured him by their favours, when he asserts that for splendour of marine and picturesque scenery, the salubrity of the air, luxury in bathing, and select society, Hastings and its environs stand unrivalled. To the invalid the locality of High-street has been particularly recommended by the faculty, for its sheltered position from the keen effects of the northerly and easterly winds. The Swan is situate within one minute's walk of the Parade.

Dinners for large or small Parties promptly and tastefully served.

A market ordinary every Saturday, at half-past One.

The spacious Assembly Room, with the Refreshment and suite of Ante-rooms, have been fitted up in a very elegant style, and are replete with every convenience for Concerts, Balls, Lectures, or Public Meetings.

A carefully-selected and well assorted stock of the most choice and delicate Wines, Piquant Liqueurs, and well-supplied Larder.

Excellent Stabling and Lock-up Coach-houses.
POST HORSES, WITH CARRIAGES OF EVERY DESCRIPTION.
Ladies' and Gentlemen's Saddle Horses,
WITH ATTENDANCE OF RIDING MASTER IF REQUIRED.
PAIR AND SINGLE PONY PHAETONS.
Royal Mail Omnibuses from the Swan Hotel to and from every Train.

Diplock's Guide 1855

Although the Swan enjoyed a considerable measure of popularity during the mid-19th century, it had become a social island in a sea of deprivation and squalor. A survey of the town's drains and sewers in 1849 revealed a festering slum with residents suffering the worst of conditions. Overflowing cesspools were being discharged on to the beach and only a third of houses had running water, but even this was contaminated by sewerage. The bulk of the population lived in overcrowded, insanitary conditions without toilets, proper drainage or clean running water.

This was bad news for tourism and for visitors to the town. The town's public health was recognised as a disaster when 65 deaths were recorded from a cholera outbreak in 1849. Many more went unrecorded.[30]

FOR SALE BY AUCTION, BY
MR. BOYKETT BREEDS,
At the SWAN HOTEL, Hastings, on THURSDAY, April 18th, at two o'clock in the afternoon precisely, by order of the proprietors,—

450 DOZENS OF WINES, comprising Port, Sherry, Madeira, Hock, Amontillado, Champagne, Claret, and Tokay; 100 Bottles (2 gallons each) fine old Cognac BRANDY; 6½ dozens Duke of Norfolk PUNCH; 6 hhds. fine old Cognac BRANDY in bond.

The quality of these Wines, Brandies, &c., will be found to be such as cannot fail to please the purchaser. Samples will be produced at the sale-room on the day of sale. A deposit of 25 per cent. to be paid to the Auctioneer at the time of sale, and which will be held by him till the Lots are delivered and found to correspond with the samples, when the remaining 75 per cent. shall be paid, except on the hogsheads of Brandy, which must be tested at the Docks and taken-to by the purchaser where they now lie. The whole of the Bottled Wines, &c., will be sold in 2 and 3 doz. Lots.

For further particulars, apply to the Auctioneer, 67, George-street, Hastings, and the Wines, &c., can be tasted at his office the day previous to the day of sale.

Wine Auction at the Swan 1850

SWAN

In this context the middle classes fled. They were followed by commercial and civic facilities including the Post Office, many shops and professional services which moved into the new town centre being built in and around Robertson Street.

Ironically, in the same year (1849), it was reported in the *Sussex Express* that 'the Swan Assembly Room has been enlarged and very handsomely fitted up.' But dimensions were not given.

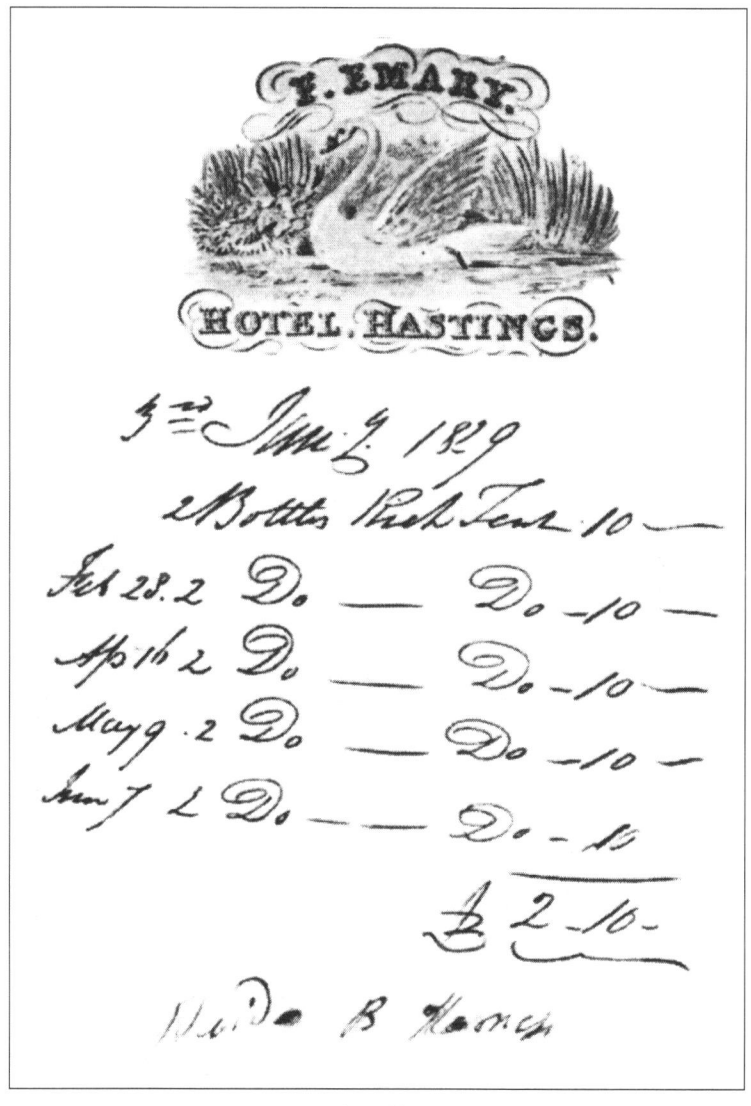

Drinks Bill 1829

SWAN

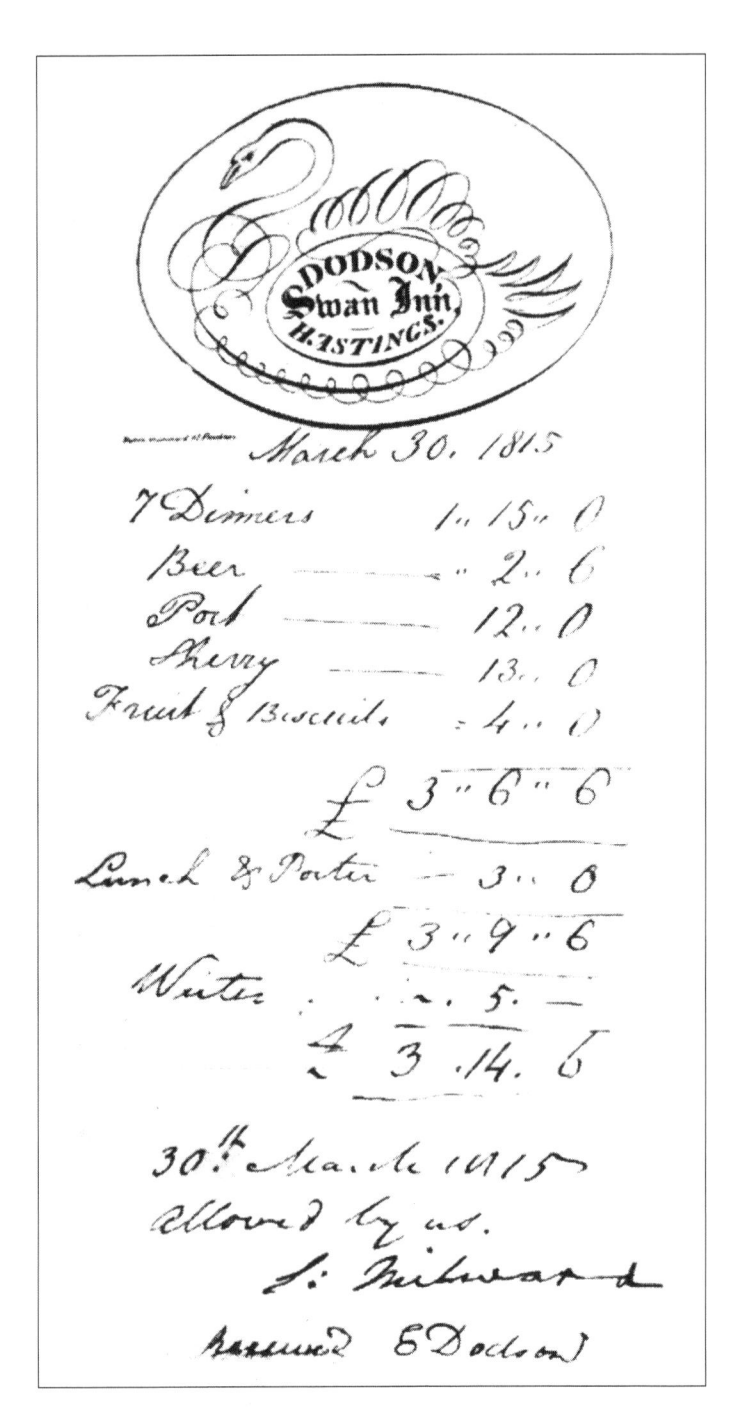

**DODSON
Swan Inn
HASTINGS.**

March 30. 1815

7 Dinners	1.. 15.. 0
Beer	-.. 2.. 6
Port	12.. 0
Sherry	13.. 0
Fruit & Biscuits	= 4.. 0

£ 3 .. 6 .. 6

Lunch & Porter — 3 .. 0

£ 3 .. 9 .. 6

Waiter ... 5. —

£ 3 .14. 6

30th March 1815
Allowed by us.
S. Milward
Received E Dodson

Hotel Bill 1815

SWAN

CHAPTER SEVEN

OLD FRIENDLY SOCIETY

Typical Nineteenth Century Friendly Society

Many clubs and societies met at the Swan during the 18th and 19th centuries. In 1757 for example, there is a report of a Sunday Nights Club meeting there, and in 1831 the Hastings Literary and Scientific Institution began in the Swan with 10 members, later growing to over 100.

This Society seems to have been of the opinion that the middle classes were at a disadvantage in educational opportunity and in 1841 the secretary wrote: '… the Lower Classes of this town have Parochial, National, British and Endowed Schools for their improvement and the young men, the Mechanics Institute, and other classes have a Book Society and Public Libraries. The Middle Classes should support this Institution as peculiarly their own, in order that they may possess equal means of acquiring useful and rational information.'

SWAN

But the organisation which became the longest established society meeting at the Swan was a benefit society known as the Old Friendly or the Hastings Friendly Society. Formed in 1815 it met regularly at the Swan until the 1880s. The society was formed 'to raise money for the mutual relief of members in old age and sickness' and 'if any member be cast into prison for debt every member should pay a penny each towards his upkeep'.

Admission was strict. 'No person remarkable for swearing, cursing, blaspheming, quarrelling, fighting and drunkenness or any other vicious or disorderly courses ... shall be admitted ….' Members were fined if they: 'Sat down in the club room before paying their quarterly money, for not attending a members funeral, for not wearing a hatband or gloves at a members funeral, for swearing or gaming in the club room', etc.

The Old Friendly was the first of many similar societies in the town, and met quarterly at the Swan for over 70 years. The most important day in the society's annual calendar was Whit Monday when, with other societies, they paraded around Hastings with bands, banners, flags, sashes and regalia. This was followed by the Annual General Meeting, and then a sumptuous dinner with speeches and rejoicing in the Assembly Room.

Other friendly societies with headquarters at other public houses, joined them on these joyous parades. They included a branch of the Oddfellows from the Kings Head, and the Benevolent Society from the Anchor. Throughout the 19th century this was a major annual event where benefit societies and later, other organisations, came together at Whitsun. Brett caught the mood in verse:-

> Whit Monday arrived and an annual sight
> filled those in the street with transient delight,
> the Friendly Society then marching past,
> with music and banners midst sightseer's vast.

Like other societies, the Old Friendly employed its own doctor (Dr Peter MacCabe). The services of Dr MacCabe were available to members during illness, and were, along with sickness payments, administered by the society as an early form of private health insurance. Many doctors in the 19th century got their living, at least

WHITSUNTIDE IN HASTINGS

Once a year, on a certain day called Whit-Monday, our ancient town springs up from its usual appearance of lethargy; the bells are set a-ringing; flags are hunted up from obscurity, and made to brave—not the battle, but the breeze; the shutters are left to keep guard over the shop-windows; the houses are emptied; the streets are thronged; carts, gigs, and chaises, come pouring in from the surrounding country, with precious freights of blooming lasses and buxom swains; and all Hastings, in a very determined and laudable spirit of independence, seems resolved to give itself a holiday.

It is ten o'clock. The principal streets are all in a commotion. The benefit societies are forming for procession. Here is the Friendly Society, collecting its members opposite the Swan hotel, there is the Manchester Unity forming its ranks by the King's Head, while the Benevolent Society, of auspicious title, raises its standard at the Anchor. The names are called over, the flags are raised, the ranks are formed, the music sounds, and the three societies form one long procession, which proceeds across the Fishmarket, up All Saints-street, to Hastings Lodge, through the grounds of F. North, Esq., by the picturesque Belmont, down the crowded High-street, to the church of St. Clement's; the paraphernalia are left outside, the three societies enter at the three doors, and at half-past eleven the service commences, terminating with a sermon from the rector. The noise and bustle of the day seem to rest for a while. One benefit society, of modern date, bearing the business-like title of the "South of England Assurance Institution," sets the solitary example of sitting down to a snug dinner, at the Hastings Arms, without any previous display for the entertainment of the holiday folks. Their dinner is nevertheless public, so that those who wish to see them had better go and dine with them. At half-past one, the bells ring out, the clubs emerge from the ancient pile, the ranks are formed, the flags regained, the music resumed, the procession re-formed, and all begins again. Off they march, down to the Fishmarket, then to the "right about," along the Parade to the further end of the town, then round the aristocratic regions of Wellington-square, and through Castle-street. On approaching the entrance to George-street, the societies pass through certain ingenious evolutions, by which means the

SWAN

> Benevolent Society is changed from the rear to the van, and proceeds to the Anchor inn, where it opens its ranks to allow the other societies to pass through, and then strikes its colours to the demands of appetite, and enters its inn to partake of what must prove a very acceptable dinner. The Friendly Society now leads the way to the Swan, where it opens it ranks to allow the Manchester Unity to pass through, and then enters its headquarters to commence an attack upon the produce of the *cuisine;* the Manchester gentlemen proceeding to the King's Head on the same laudable errand.

The Hastings & St Leonards News 16.06.1848

in part, by administering to the medical needs of the members of friendly societies.

Dr MacCabe was integrated into the society and was expected to march with them on Whit Monday parades, to report back at society meetings and to attend soirées and the Annual General Meeting. He was paid the relatively small sum of 10 guineas a year, which compared, for example, to the Adelaide Lodge of Oddfellows in St Leonards, was a measly sum. The Oddfellows paid their doctor a very handsome £80. But Dr MacCabe was a publicly spirited Irishman who saw his work as a contribution to the community. He was twice Mayor in 1838 and 1843 when he seconded an appeal for relief of the Irish famine.

In 1847 The Friendly Society was taken to court by one of its members who had been refused relief when he was sick and unable to work. I paraphrase the newspaper report: 'The member, Henry Whyborn, had been driving a cart load of lime from Eastbourne to Hastings when he had the misfortune to be thrown from the cart, and became jammed between the waggon and a post at the bottom of Glynde Lane in Bexhill. It was found that his leg was broken and he was obliged to submit to amputation.'

The cause of the accident was due to the horses being young and frisky and being easily frightened by the noise of a steam engine on the newly built railroad. The Friendly Society had, without any evidence, alleged that Whyborn was drunk at the time of the accident. One of their rules stated that if a member met with an accident while drunk, he should not be entitled to relief.'

SWAN

> **RYE.—EASTER MONDAY.**—We had quite a gala day here; the Hastings Friendly Society, which formed a branch here some time ago, having got up an excursion to visit us. The train arrived about three o'clock in the afternoon, bringing about 400 persons, and accompanied by an excellent brass band. They were met at the station by the members of the branch society, and followed by a large concourse of spectators, amid the jocund ringing of bells and firing of cannon. The whole formed in procession and perambulated the principal streets of the town. They waited upon the Mayor, to whom the committee presented a copy of the rules of the society, and afterwards drank the health of his worship and wife. They then proceeded to the Hope and Anchor Inn, where a spacious booth had been erected. The inner man having been refreshed, dancing commenced and was kept up with great spirit until six o'clock. At this period Mr. H. Polhill took the chair, Mr. James Thomas officiating as vice. After a great many excellent speeches and songs, the company broke up at nine o'clock, the visitors being accompanied to the station by their Rye friends and loudly cheered as they took their departure.

Sussex Express 14.4.1854

Whyborn continued his journey to the sluice at Pevensey. He stopped at the Sluice public house and had some beer. After refreshment he continued through the marsh to Bexhill calling at a second public house. He then travelled through Bexhill stopping at the railroad as a train approached. The two young horses shied, and Whyborn's endeavour to stop them forced the waggon against a post, and crushed his leg. There he lay until picked up by Mr Wallis, a surgeon of Bexhill, who was passing in a fly, and who brought him to Hastings.'

Whyborn made a claim for relief but the committee ignored the claim and refused to assess his condition. They didn't ask him to account for the charge brought against him and he had therefore no other resource but the law.' All of the witnesses including the doctor who assisted him and operated on his leg, gave evidence in his favour and against the society. The court decided there was no case to justify the refusal of relief and the committee were obliged to make the payments accordingly.'

By 1855 the original membership of 13 had grown to 739 making it the largest friendly society in Hastings, with a branch in Rye. But although the society had capital funds of over £3,000, it suffered from the downward cycle of the economy and from a miscalculation of investment. Subsequently it experienced difficulty paying out the sick benefits, funeral grants and annuities claimed by its ageing membership.

In 1856 the treasurer, a member of the society for 40 years, was accused by the secretary of robbing the society of £30, and he was excluded from membership. When asked to return the £30 he went to court to prove his innocence. After a long case and with all the details being examined, the Mayor said that the society had not made out a sufficient case why he should be expelled, and that he be reinstated.

After this, membership went into decline but managed to continue until at least 1880 with a reduced membership of 412. It may of moved to the Old Town Hall where a 'Hastings Friendly Society' met in 1884. But whether or not this was the same society is unknown. Thomas Brett 'thought the society would flourish until the end of time', but stated it became moribund even before the old Swan was demolished in 1889.

By this time Hastings had dozens of various sick and benefit societies spread around the town. The vast majority operated mainly, but not exclusively, from public houses.

The long room at the Swan Shades, a tap room attached to the Swan, was also used by another friendly society. The Regency Lodge of Oddfellows which, as its name implies, was established during the regency of the Prince of Wales, afterwards George IV. On its anniversary, the 22nd August, its members perambulated the town with their regalia which included a pair of globes, afterwards dining together in their lodge room. The 'long room' or 'lodge room' is not shown on any ground plan, so it is assumed it was on the first floor.

In 1840 the Oddfellows held their annual ball in the lodge room with nearly 200 in attendance. 'The room was splendidly decorated upon the occasion. The guests sat down to a substantial supper which did great credit to Mr Farrol, the landlord, as did also his wines and spirits. The party did not separate till the dawn of morning.'

SWAN

CHAPTER EIGHT

SWAN AT PLAY

Eighteenth century cockpit

In 1769 the *Kentish Gazette* advertised that Abraham Smith organised at the George Inn, Rye, the Bulls Head, Battle and the Swan, Hastings, a cockfighting tournament with 11 cocks in each of two teams. The stakes were four guineas [£4.20] for each of 10 fights and 10 guineas [£10.50] for the final battle. As was common in those times each of these venues must have had their own cockpit. In the case of the Swan this was probably located in an outbuilding in the Swan yard.

Among the major entertainers who appeared and performed at the Swan Assembly Room over the years were many musicians, singers, comedians and actors — some on tour, some local. Brett reported that: '1814 was one of the most crowded seasons within the memory of the then inhabitants of Hastings. The Swan was literally overflowing with good company. A celebrated ventriloquist named Charles gave a week's performance in the Swan Assembly Room where fashionable meetings were said to be numerically the largest ever known!'

When a new licensee, George Robinson, arrived in 1839, 50 members of the Swan Harmonic Society sang at his opening dinner. They were followed by the Hastings Old Band. The Swan Harmonic Society held weekly harmonic meetings where members 'smoked a pipe, had a pot or two and sang together', but on occasion they also danced. A favourite 19th century dance was the quadrille, a square dance for eight people in four couples.

An esteemed entertainer was Arthur Bolingbroke, a popular local pianist and highly complimented tenor and composer of quadrilles. His version of *Sally in our Alley* and other ballads it was said, 'evoked unstinted applause even from the most critical'.

THE SHAPCOTT FAMILY,

As they appeared at the Theatre Royal Drury Lane, London, October 28, 1850.

Memorable entertainment was also provided by 'Joseph Shapcott and his Seven Unrivalled Sons' who, in 1850 performed two Saxhorn Concerts of opera and other pieces. The Saxhorn, a brass instrument with valves similar to the flugelhorn, was a new instrument at the time. The youngest son was a five-year-old drummer who performed the solo part of a drum polka. The band was conducted and accompanied by William Handley on the Cornet-A-Piston and on the Cornopeon, both now obsolete names for the cornet.

The Inhabitants and Visitors of
HASTINGS, ST. LEONARDS, AND THEIR VICINITIES,
Are respectfully informed that
MR. J. SHAPCOTT,
(OF EXETER,)
And his Seven Unrivalled Sons,
WILL GIVE
TWO GRAND SACRED AND CLASSICAL
SAX-HORN CONCERTS,
AT
THE SWAN ASSEMBLY ROOM, HASTINGS,
On Monday and Tuesday Evenings,
NOVEMBER 18*th* and 19*th*, 1850.

Mr. SHAPCOTT has engaged the services of that Eminent Performer on the
CORNET A PISTON,
MR. W. H. HANDLEY,
Of the Royal Italian Opera, &c., &c., &c.
Who will, during the Evening, Conduct and Perform some of those Brilliant Embellishments upon the *CORNOPEAN*, which have been received with such raptures throughout Europe.

SWAN

It was announced that 'between the parts of each evening Mr Shapcott will deliver short addresses on musical education etc. and narrate the circumstances of his success in cultivating the talent of music to such perfection in his family'.

A second musical prodigy to perform at the Swan was another five-year-old, this time an Irish girl known as the Infant Lyra, who performed on the harp 'with such extraordinary ability that Swan audiences were absolutely astonished'.

A popular artist was John Parry. Described as a musical humorist, John Parry gave 'racy performances at the Swan Assembly Rooms before fashionable and overflowing audiences'. One sketch billed as 'Notes Vocal and Instrumental', was an act which caused 'fervid, enthusiastic applause and great bursts of laughter'.

Another sketch was 'The Piano taught in Six Lessons', where Parry presented various portraits of Victorian ladies and gentlemen learning to play the piano. The 'Ornamental Young Lady' was one. The 'Gent who was never certain about the right key' and 'The young man who thought himself an artist' were others. It was reported that Parry created huge roars of laughter, and at the end of the evening 'the large audiences left the Swan in delighted conversation and with risibility on their faces'. John Parry had few equals in the Assembly Room.

A somewhat different entertainment organised within the Swan but taking place outside of it, featured a local butcher called John Rayner who had no equal as an athlete in Hastings, and who attempted a series of running feats in the district. A popular event was a timed run from Hastings to Rye and back, a distance of 21 miles run in under three hours. Another event was a sprint from the Hare and Hounds, Ore to the Swan in under five minutes. These events attracted huge crowds and the Swan became a temporary betting shop. Some wagers were placed for very large sums of money at great odds.

Another long distance runner was Laurence Glyde (1814–1911) who raced the stage coaches from the Swan Inn to London — a distance of more than 60 miles. Starting at the Swan he caught up with the coach, when the horses were being changed along the route. He always arrived in London before the coach.

SWAN

PROGRAMME.
FIRST EVENING.

First Part.

Holy, Holy,	Handel.
Calcutta, (arranged by Master Theophilus Shapcott.)	
While Shepherds Watch, (Anthem.)	
The Heavens are telling,	Haydn.
Hallelujah Chorus	Handel.

Second Part.

Selection from the Stabat Mater,	Rosseau.
Vital Spark,	Harwood.
The Marvellous Works,	Haydn.
Sound the Loud Timbrel,	Avison.
National Anthem,	Dr. Bull.

Drum Polka, in which **Master Frank Shapcott, a Child only 5 years old,** will Perform the Solo Part.

SECOND EVENING.

First Part.

...al ever...	Earl of Mornington.
Selection ...cira,	Bellini.
When thy Bosom,	Braham.
March in Norma,	S. Lover.
The Guard Ship,	
A Grand Selection from Anna Boleyna,	Donnizetti.

Second Part.

Overture to Italiano in Algieria,	Rossini.
The Drum Polka, (Master Frank, &c.)	Jullien.
I know a Bank,	Horn.
Selection from Lucia de Lammermoor	Donnezetti.
National Anthem,	Dr. Bull.

Between the Parts on each Evening,

MR. SHAPCOTT
Will Deliver Short Addresses on Musical Education, &c.

And narrate the circumstances of his success in cultivating the Talent of Music to such perfection in his Family.

The following is but the echo of the opinions of thousands in England and Scotland, who have listened to this extraordinary Family.

JERSEY, MONDAY, AUGUST 26th, 1850.

"Being desirous that my family and pupils should have the gratification of listening to the far-famed *Sax-Horn Band*, I desired Mr. SHAPCOTT to attend with his Sons at Sion House, to give us a private Concert. The satisfaction they gave was universal, and a higher or a more intellectual and improving treat I think it is impossible for young people to have. The music was of the best kind, the *execution surpassingly brilliant, and the effect thrilling in the extreme.* In point of effect, I have never listened to instruments that can produce any thing at all approaching to it."—ELIAS NEAL, Principal of ...

"The *Sax-Horn Band* is a perfect novelty, and when arranged in the order in which the various members of it appear before an audience, might make a capital subject for a painter. Even before the auditory nerves receive the several and bewitching impressions of their mingling intonations, the eye seems to become sensible of a harmony and suitableness in their dispositions, varying from manhood to a child of five years old; but when the full cadence bursts upon the ear, and the mellow concords float through the spacious Hall, the thrilling emotions awakened in the soul, were such as only good music properly performed could produce. The '*March in Norma*,' in which the solo was sustained by Master Thomas Shapcott, a child nine years old, was brilliant in every respect."—WEST OF ENGLAND CONSERVATIVE.

Admission Tickets, 1s. each.   Reserved Seats, 2s.

May be had at HASTINGS, of Mr. ELFORD, Music Seller, George Street; at Messrs. DIPLOCK and REID's Libraries; and of Mr. F. BECK, 3, George Street; also, at Mr. E. HOLT's Library, White Rock; and at St. Leonards, of Mr. J. BECK, 44, Marina, and Mr. R. COLEMAN, Grand Parade.

Doors open each Evening at half-past 7 o'clock. Concert to commence at 8.

No. 14 of THE ABSTINENCE STANDARD and MORAL REFORMER,—PRICE ONE PENNY, contains an ENGRAVING and BIOGRAPHICAL SKETCH of the SHAPCOTT FAMILY. The STANDARD is Published in London, every Saturday, W. HORSELL, 13, Paternoster Row, and W. TWEEDIE, 11, Wellington Street North, Strand; also of Mr. F. BECK, 3, Street, Hastings.

Programme 1850

> What dinners, what dances, what shows and what games have here been engaged in by grand-dads and dames.

Thomas Brandon Brett

Mesmerism and Clairvoyance.

SWAN ASSEMBLY ROOMS, Hastings,

At Eight o'clock THIS EVENING, Friday, May 3 ; also on Saturday Morning, May 4, at Two o'clock, and again in the Evening at Eight o'clock.

PROFESSOR EAGLE begs most respectfully to call public attention to the arrangements he has made

FOR A SHORT PERIOD

at the above Rooms, for affording persons of every class an evening's amusement of such an unexceptionable character as must recommend itself to all those who are fond of the marvellous ; while to the contemplative mind it opens a wide field of thought at the cunning of human art, and the far more mysterious properties of nature.

Mr. EAGLE has been known throughout the United Kingdom as a Professor of Legerdemain, and in order to present an attractive evening's entertainment, he purposes giving

A GRAND MYSTIC SOIREE,

during which much is to *be* seen, but more *not* to be seen.

This first part of the performance to conclude with the

INEXHAUSTIBLE BOTTLE,

from which 100 glasses of whiskey, brandy, gin, rum, ale, &c., &c., may be obtained.

This trick was successfully played before Her Majesty at Balmoral Castle, in Scotland.

MESMERISM AND CLAIRVOYANCE.

Professor EAGLE would more particularly call attention to the extraordinary properties of mind displayed by his daughter, MISS GEORGIANA EAGLE, the CELEBRATED CLAIRVOYANT, who, although but fifteen years of age, has, while in the mesmeric state, shown an intimate acquaintance with SCIENCE, HISTORY, POLITICS, RELIGION, &c., &c.—the past—present—and future ;—her mind not only being carried with the rapidity of thought over the extent of the earth's surface, but giving explicit answers to questions put by the audience relative to the condition of parties far distant.

This is no exaggeration, but TRUTH—bearing out the principle expressed in the adage—" Truth is stranger than fiction."

Tickets to be had at the Libraries and the Swan Hotel, Hastings. Reserved seats 2s. 6d.—second 1s. 6d.—back ditto 1s.

SWAN

CHAPTER NINE

SWAN AT WORK

Little is recorded about the many people who worked at the Swan over the centuries, but in the Registers of St Clements Church, Brett found a record that in March 1609 there was buried in the churchyard, 'one John, Ostler at the Swan'.

Another ostler, Thomas Newman, suffered an awful death by scalding many years later in 1756. Further details on how this tragedy occurred and how his life came to such a terrible end is unknown but it was most likely an accident in the brew house.

Sixty years later in 1816, the stage coach booking clerks were William Nabbs and John Lavender. One of the ostlers at that time was Tom Barham. In 1836 William Whiteman, a pauper who had become 'a burden on the rates', was ordered to be removed to the parish of his birth. In his defence it was stated that he had agreed with landlord Thomas Stockwell in 1809 'to serve as a potboy for one year'.[31] In 1845 James Foster, later to become well known as a proprietor of the Public Hall, was a waiter at the Swan.

Various occupations of employees who lived in are listed in the census. The usual female occupations of house keeper, chambermaid, kitchen maid, housemaid, barmaid and cook are listed, as well as the male occupations of boots, under boots, hotel porter, billiard marker, tapster (bar tender), waiter and potboy. Before the introduction of the beer engine (the pump on the bar), the potboy had to bring the beer up from the cellar.

The head ostler for many years in the mid-19th century was John Duly. The Duly family lived and worked from their house, now Ostler's Cottage in Swan Avenue.

The transport of goods between Hastings and other towns and cities using fly vans and waggons, by a number of carriers, operated from the Swan for at least 200 years. Tilden Smith for example, provided a regular carrier service from the Swan and Crown Inns in the early 1820s. He made three journeys a week to the White Hart and Spur Inns, Borough, changing horses at inns along the way. He also delivered goods – particularly on market days – to towns and villages around East Sussex. By the mid-1820s he also operated a timber business from the Swan, supplied by boats owned by Breeds, which unloaded on Hastings beach. He probably employed men in saw pits. He is mentioned in a deed as having a part interest in the Swan freehold, and by 1829 he was the licensee of the John's Cross in Robertsbridge.

Wheelwright at Work

Other occupations, including the trades of blacksmith, wheelwright and carriage repairer, were located in the Swan yard and in Hill Street from at least the 1700s. At that time much of the street was owned by the Breeds family. They owned the land which became 'the site of a blacksmith's shop, forge and warehouse, formerly in the occupation of William Sparrow tenant of Sarah Breeds, the elder',[32] and later occupied by William Woolgar, blacksmith, who also had a

SWAN

beer house called the Blacksmiths Arms at the bottom of All Saints Street.

Blacksmiths were employed at the Swan to shoe the extensive number of horses that either belonged to the Swan stables or were brought in by their private owners. Likewise the carriage repairers who refurbished the phaetons, chariots, gigs and other horse-drawn vehicles, also worked here. Wheelwrights were employed to 'shrink' metal tyres onto the cart wheels and to strengthen the hubs. Blacksmiths kept a fire going throughout the day and late afternoon, and at the end of the day the hot coals were scooped up and taken to bakers' ovens for baking bread overnight. It is probable that the Swan had, at one time, its own bakehouse.

Blacksmith at Work

SWAN

Swan yard 1870s

SWAN

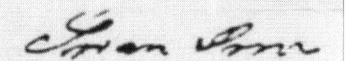

HASTINGS AND LONDON
FLY VANS
AND
OLD-ESTABLISHED WAGGON,
TO THE
White Hart and Spur Inns, Boro'
By TILDEN SMITH.

VANS set out every Saturday, Tuesday, and Thursday Evenings, from the Crown and Swan Coach Offices, Hastings, arrive at the White Hart Inn, Boro' every Tuesday, Thursday, and Saturday. A WAGGON sets out every Saturday and arrives at the Spur Inn every Wednesday.

Invoice 1825

SWAN

Nineteenth century photo of Swan Hotel

SWAN

CHAPTER TEN

SWAN SHADES

Swan Hotel with Swan Shades far right of picture

Meanwhile the Swan Shades, a second licensed premises within the estate, catered for working-class customers, employees of the hotel and yard, and the servants of Swan patrons. This building on the corner of Hill Street and Swan Terrace was originally the location of a small brew house, a school house and most likely St Clements Chantry and garden.

From 1727 the Swan was occupied by a widow, Mrs Mercy Grove, one of the original brewsters or alewives. In 1728 she married business partner Richard Halstead and when he died she carried on running the Swan alone until 1747 when she issued the following notice:-

SWAN

> To be sold immediately, the Swan Inn, with Brewery, Stabling, two Gardens etc, enquire of Widow Halstead in Hastings.

Thomas Breeds was Swan landlord from about 1751 to 1771. Another Thomas Breeds was a partner in the first Hastings Bank, which in 1812 purchased the Swan and the house on the corner of Swan Terrace and Hill Street, from Edward Millward, for £9,000. The corner house is described in another deed as 'on the site whereof a brew house formerly stood commonly called the School House ... in occupation of Mary Pitman then Richard Piper'.[33] This suggests it could be the site of the original chantry.

In 1812 the corner house was then known as the Swan Tap and by 1816 as the Swan Shades. The Hastings Bank sold the Swan to Edward Wenham in 1820 but there was no further mention of

Swan Shades

the brew house. Brett mentions the Swan brewing its own beer in 1832, but does not give his source.

In 1836 William Eldridge, described as an innkeeper and brick maker, previously proprietor of the Saxon Hotel and Shades, St Leonards, purchased the Swan for about £8,000 with two mortgages. The low price reflected the fact that the Swan was in need of refurbishment. Eldridge quickly built several new coach houses and stables and implemented an improvement plan for the whole estate. Also he probably opened up a second coach entrance in Hill Street shown on an undated plan drawn between 1840 and 1855.

Eldridge spent a considerable sum of money fitting up the hotel in a luxurious manner with furnishings and drapery provided by Clement and Inskipp, a local furniture company of repute. At this time the Swan had no less than six 'Parlors' on the ground floor serviced by waiters from a bar inside the hotel lobby. It is interesting to note that the Swan used the Anglo-French spelling 'parlor' rather than the English 'parlour', indicating a semi-private lounge for relaxation and conversation and a place where men went to smoke fashionable clay pipes and to read the London and county papers, which were delivered on horseback and by coach.

Eldridge applied to the Hastings Improvement Commissioners to lower the raised Oak Hill pavement to street level so that patrons of the Swan 'could have an uninterrupted (passage) along the High Street … on a continuous paved footway'.[34] He also asked for permission to remove the distinctive portico which projected three feet over the footpath at the main hotel entrance. But neither was agreed. In addition he resurfaced the extensive Swan yard, much improving its previous muddy condition. The Hastings Improvement Commissioners followed suit and 'macadamised' the High Street.

However, because of excessive borrowing and spending, by mid-1837 Eldridge was declared bankrupt and forced to retire.[35] One of his creditors was James Rock the Hastings coachmaker, who probably owned some of the coaches franchised to the hotel. The Swan was then auctioned off by Messrs Southey and Son at Garraways Coffee House, Cornhill, London by order of the assignees.

Sometime in the 1840s it became tied or partially tied to the Bear Brewery of Lewes. The owners of the Bear Brewery, Thomas and Edward Monk, became freeholders of the Swan and had a

SWAN

Church Street

Kitchen | Bar | late Tap room | Pantry | Kitchen | Parlor
Yard | Skittle ground | Scullery | Wash Kitchen house yard | Hall | Bar

The late J Williams' premises

Coach house | Parlors

Stable

Yard

Ostler's house

Yard

Ostry | Coach office
Saddle room | Parlor
 | Shop

Stables

Oak Hill houses belonging to Mr Francis Smith

Coach house | Yard

Stables

High Street

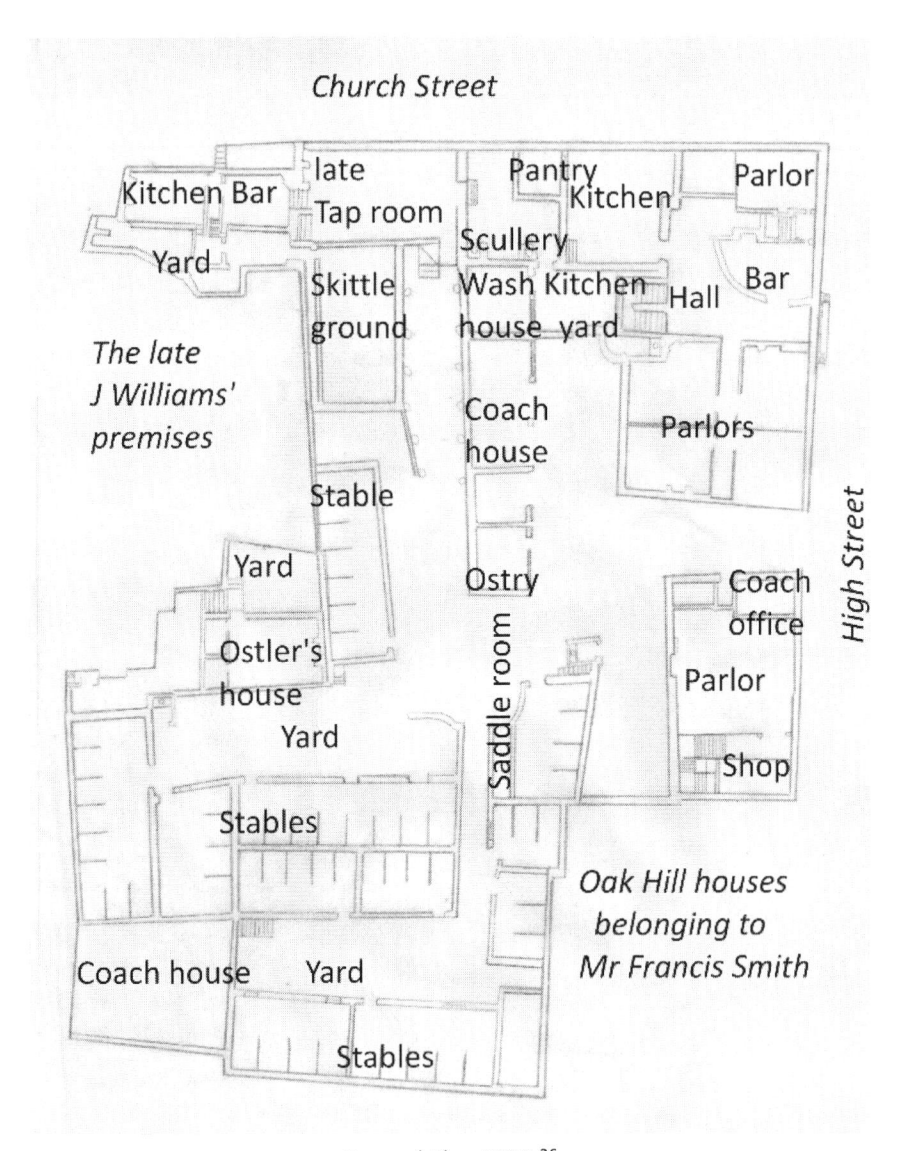

Ground Plan 1836 [36]

covenant in the deeds allowing them to supply the Swan with 'all beer, ale, porter, stout and other malt liquors *except* bottled beer, stout or draught bitter'. Who supplied bottled beer and draught bitter is unknown but Thomas and Edward Monk continued as the freeholders until 1889 when the Swan was demolished and rebuilt. The freehold, of course, included the Shades.

SWAN

The *Oxford English Dictionary* states that the term 'shades' originated in 19th century Brighton, as a synonym for wine vaults, but was also a term used elsewhere as 'oyster shades', signifying the availability of prostitutes. The government Select Committee on Public Houses in 1852, also mentioned shades, describing them as wine rooms trading under the name of the Vinters Company, and also used by prostitutes.

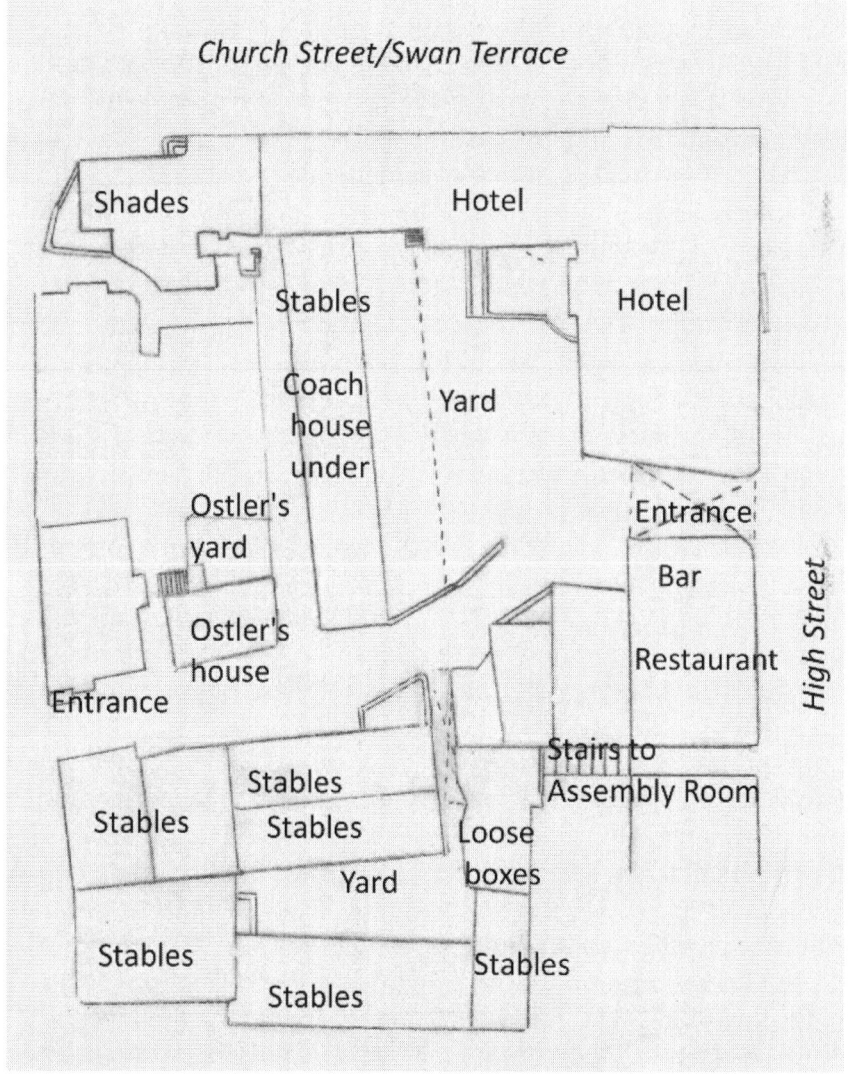

Ground plan 1840–1855 [37]

SWAN

On the south-east coast, the name 'shades' was commonly used for taprooms located behind major hotels, of which the Swan was a typical example. Other examples in Hastings included the Albion, Saxon, Castle and Queen's Hotel shades. There were many other shades attached to hotels in Eastbourne, Brighton and further inland. Some smaller public houses in Hastings also aped the idea.

Shades bars came into existence because of the demands of the military personnel billeted along the south-east coast during the Napoleonic Wars. After the Battle of Trafalgar in 1805, Napoleon directed his attention elsewhere in Europe; the threat of invasion declined and troop numbers were reduced. Military custom was then replaced by that of fashionable Victorian gentlemen then starting to patronise Hastings as an early pleasure resort.

After 1830 shades bars enabled hotel proprietors to profit from the 1830 Beer Act, to keep working-class customers and prostitution at arm's length but at the same time to discreetly supply the sexual demands of 'gentlemen customers'.[38]

The 1836 ground plan of the Swan estate shows the room in the Shades abutting Hill Street as a kitchen. The kitchen was connected by a few stairs to the bar and by a second set of stairs to a third room marked 'late tap room'. This tap room is now the site of the house or houses next door in Swan Terrace. The open space at the rear of the Shades is shown as a skittle ground with steps leading up into the Shades. This ground plan confirms that the Shades occupied a much larger area than just the corner house and was physically integrated into the hotel itself. It also confirms that there was direct access between the Shades and the hotel at ground floor level.

In the 1860s the Swan was criticised by the magistrates for letting rooms to prostitutes who congregated in the Shades. In 1865 the chief constable, dealing with a complaint about the Swan and Castle Shades, remarked: 'It is almost impossible [for landlords] to get a living without resorting to something beyond the ordinary trade', indicating the dire trading conditions then prevalent.[39] The Swan Shades is not listed in the Hastings Petty Sessions Register indicating that its landlords were under tenants of the Swan.

Meanwhile, customers of the Shades continued their unrestrained and bawdy behaviour. Brett recalled the Shades providing entertainments 'of a somewhat less pretentious character

SWAN

Silchester House, formerly Swan Shades

than those which were held at the big house'. At a fishermen's dance or 'shilling hop' held in 1857, one drinker, alias 'Spring heel Jack', who worked in a 'deeze'* curing herrings, was charged with drunken behaviour.[40]

In 1868, another customer, alias 'Captain Jinks the last Hastings highwayman', started his final journey of plunder across the southern counties of England on a horse 'borrowed' from the Swan stables. After robbing several persons on the highway he was finally arrested in Henley-on-Thames and escorted back to Hastings to face imprisonment.

In 1872 a police constable reported a drinker in the bar of the Shades for 'using language the reverse of complimentary'. The constable complained he had been threatened by the man who told him, 'I can put twenty such fellows as you under a bushel'.

Landlord Charles Griffin thought the constable was biased. 'He is always under my windows', he said. 'If he had been one of the old constables he would have said, Come now Charley, shut up and you'll hear no more about it.' Although this caused a roar of laughter in court, he was nevertheless fined five shillings [25p].[41]

* a local word for a place where herrings were cured.

SWAN

Bad behaviour in a shades bar is not unexpected. The bars of the Swan itself however were a different matter. Having gained a reputation for decorum and manners over the centuries the Swan was thought to be beyond reproach. 'There are no stories of immoderate drinking and rioting in the Swan', remarked one local historian, 'there is no reference to any disturbance there'; an unwise claim to make for a public house.[42] In 1888 a Swan customer was arrested for brawling with a prostitute in the same bar and for threatening her with a cast iron spittoon.[43]

> **SOIREE MUSICALE**.- On Tuesday evening, a general gathering of the singers of the different 'choirs of Hastings took place in Mr. Winter's large room at the Swan Shades; upwards of 80 sat down to an excellent tea. Mr J Tutt was called to the chair, while Mr Parks officiated as vice-chairman. The meeting originated with some of the members of the St Clement's choir, and the Chairman and Vice stated the objects to be, to show in an unmistakable manner that there was no ground for the belief that had got abroad, to the effect that there were differences of friendship between the choirs; and also to give their relations and friends a little musical entertainment, in proof of the progress they had made in their united class that was now meeting three times a week. It was gratifying to know that while many more alluring recreations were constantly addressing themselves to the lower desires of our young men, none of them has yet abated in his attendance at the present class. The church wardens of St Clement's had appreciated the objects of the present meeting and had kindly given ten shillings each towards it. The whole class then gave some favourite specimens from Handel's Messiah and Judas Maccabeus followed by a few glees and madrigals. After having done ample justice to the excellent viands of the obliging host, and indulged sufficiently in the pleasures of Helicon, the company at length yielded themselves up to the bewitching fascinations of Terpischore and in due time thus terminated an evening of complete enthusiasm.'

Sussex Express 26.02.1853

CHAPTER ELEVEN

JOSEPH COLLINS: A SWAN LANDLORD

Photographer: Constantine Jennings, Hastings 1881–1886

Joseph Collins married his first wife Jane in London in 1850. In 1874 he took the licence of the Swan Inn and they moved into their new home. What seems to have been a tumultuous married life came into the public light later that year.

Reading between the lines of a case at the Hastings Magistrates Court in 1874 it appears that Jane Collins was an alcoholic. The hearing followed an incident in the bar of the Swan when Mrs Collins was arrested for drunken assault after attacking her husband with a poker.

The cause of this incident remains unknown but understandably Joseph Collins was a very distressed man. The Swan at this time was the headquarters of three separate branches of Freemasons. It seems improbable that a landlord of a Masonic pub would not be a member himself. Joseph Collins would have received support from them during his ordeal.

At the start of December 1874 the case was reported in the *Hastings and St Leonards Chronicle*:-

HASTINGS BOROUGH BENCH.

A SCENE IN COURT.

JANE COLLINS, wife of the landlord of the Swan, was summoned for assaulting and threatening Joseph Collins, her husband.

Complainant informed the Bench that his wife "would not dress herself," to come.

A warrant was issued, and she was escorted to the station by a constable.

Prisoner appeared without bonnet or head dress. She was in an excited state, and frequently interrupted her husband, in giving evidence.

The Clerk asked if she was sober?

Prisoner—I am able to answer for myself.

Love, the gaoler, thought she was sober; but complainant and the Supt. thought she was not, the latter remarking that he was sure she was suffering from the effects of drink.

A sad and pitiful tale was revealed by the husband, who quite broke down in relating his complaint to the Bench. The unfortunate woman, in her madness for drink, had attacked him with a poker; and from her threats he felt that something serious would come of it. She had knocked him down that morning. He still had bruises from the blows he received with the poker.

Prisoner (excitedly)—Will you see mine, sir? The woman exhibited her arms.

Mr Collins said that the bruises she had were caused in holding her, to prevent her getting drink.

The Clerk's question—Is it caused by drink? seemed to rouse the unfortunate prisoner to fury. She shouted, "It's a lie! It's a lie," and continued to talk until she raised her voice to the highest pitch. It became evident that she was far from being "in her sober senses," and the Mayor said that, as the magistrates considered she was not in a fit state for the case to go on, she would be remanded till the next day.

Prisoner—You will let me go home, sir?

The Mayor—No, you must remain here.

The unfortunate woman poured out a torrent of abuse on her husband, using foul language. She had to be removed from the dock by force.

Hastings & St Leonards Chronicle 2.12.1874

SWAN

The case continued the following day and Jane Collins was 'bound over in three sureties' of £25 each for six months. She was required to deposit £25 herself and to find two others willing to do the same. This was a lot of money – in today's value about £3,400 – but as she didn't raise that amount she was imprisoned in Lewes Gaol for two and a half weeks. She was then bound over again 'in two sureties to keep the peace towards her husband for six months'.

Jane Collins died in 1880 and her husband buried her in London. The following year he got remarried to Mary Jane Winter, a much younger woman who was the daughter of George Reeves Winter and Jane Winter who ran another Hastings pub, the Hope Inn, at Halton (1865–1876).

Joseph and Mary Jane Collins had three sons born in 1882, 1884 and 1887. The first two were born in the Swan and Herbert had the middle name of 'Carswell' after the previous Swan licensees William and Elizabeth Carswell to whom they may have been related. William Carswell was also a 'brother mason'.

All three sons eventually emigrated to America where their descendants reside to this day and where Charles was an active Mason. When the oldest son Herbert died in 1966 his ashes were returned to England and deposited in Hastings Cemetery with his mother and father. It is a family belief that "his heart never left England".

Recently Joseph Collins (2), of New York, the great-grandson of Joseph Collins (1) visited Hastings with his wife Luanne in search of their family roots.

In Joseph's own words:-

> My grandfather and the middle son were buried here in the States and before our first trip to England in 2009, I asked all living relatives, if they knew where the oldest son was buried. He had lived in Illinois, so all parties assumed he was buried there. In 2009 I went to Hastings Cemetery to look up a family lot number that was left behind in a family photo album, and in the office, there in one of the old record books, was the family: Joseph and Mary Jane, her father and mother, and Joseph and Mary Jane's oldest son and his wife. Records showed the son and his wife were cremated, so shipping from the States would have been less expensive I assume. Also, the office said that the area of the grave lot was void of grave

SWAN

Mary Jane & Joseph Collins with Charles, Ivor and Herbert

stones, as they'd removed them decades ago in the 1950s. They said they had put ads in the papers, so anyone wanting their stone kept could apply, and those stones would stay. Only two stones are lying on the ground at the entrance to the site. The office staff said how far apart the lots were, and where my family plot was in relation to the front gate, so we went to the site and sure enough, only roses, no stones, except the two. I started at the gate pacing off three feet at a time, to get to the second row, then turned and started down the row, counting off three feet for each pace. As I got about ten feet from where I would stop, I noticed a little stone in the lawn and it happened to be where my counting would end up. I looked at the stone and it had sunk down a bit and grass had grown over a lot of it, but I could make out the name 'Collins'. I tore back the grass and there were the names of my grand-uncle and grand-aunt. I had found them.[44]

Hastings Cemetery

Joseph and Mary Jane gave up the Swan in 1884 five years before the old inn was demolished. In a report of 1889 he was described as a man 'remembered by thousands', suggesting at least that he was a very popular landlord.

SWAN

Joseph and Luanne Collins, Ithaca, New York 2013

Headed notepaper

SWAN

CHAPTER TWELVE

SWAN DEMOLISHED AND REBUILT

The declining fortunes of the Swan continued throughout the 1870s and 1880s, until it was obvious the business was in need of some rationalisation. This was amply indicated by the fact that there were only two guests in this 40 bedroomed hotel on census night 1881. Both were merchant travellers, that is travelling salesmen.

However, the Swan was not alone. Economic conditions in the last 30 years of the 19th century affected many other hotels in the town. The Havelock and the Royal Albion for example, both closed as hotels at this time, as did the Marine on Marine Parade (now Pelham Place). The Palace hotel actually opened in 1887 but experienced immediate financial difficulties. The Mayor of Hastings attempted to give some support to the ailing Swan by reviving the Mayor's Annual Banquet there in 1885, but the downward spiral continued.

In 1884 John Plowman, described as a swimming bath proprietor from Oxford, obtained the lease and the licence. He died in 1886 and his widow then ran the Swan for a year before handing over to Joseph Bullman, a tailor and outfitter from Ashford.[45] Bullman's short time as landlord was dogged by more bad luck and bad trade, and in March 1888 the Swan was the subject of an auction with a reserve price of £7,000. The schedule included 'the hotel, shades, restaurant, outbuildings, yards, coach houses, boxes for 50 horses, lofts over, granaries, a harness room and a head ostler's house';[46] also a former wheelwright's shop, forge and warehouse in Hill Street, and 'part of the stockroom, bar and restaurant, formerly part of a shop adjoining the entrance to the ball room staircase' from the High Street.

There was a large attendance of brewers, publicans and others at the auction. Thomas Turner landlord of the Globe Hotel, Queen's Road bid £4,500. William Freeman landlord of the Norman bid £5,000 but the highest bid at £6,400 meant it remained unsold, although the auctioneer teased the audience with jokes about 'this little goldmine'.

SWAN

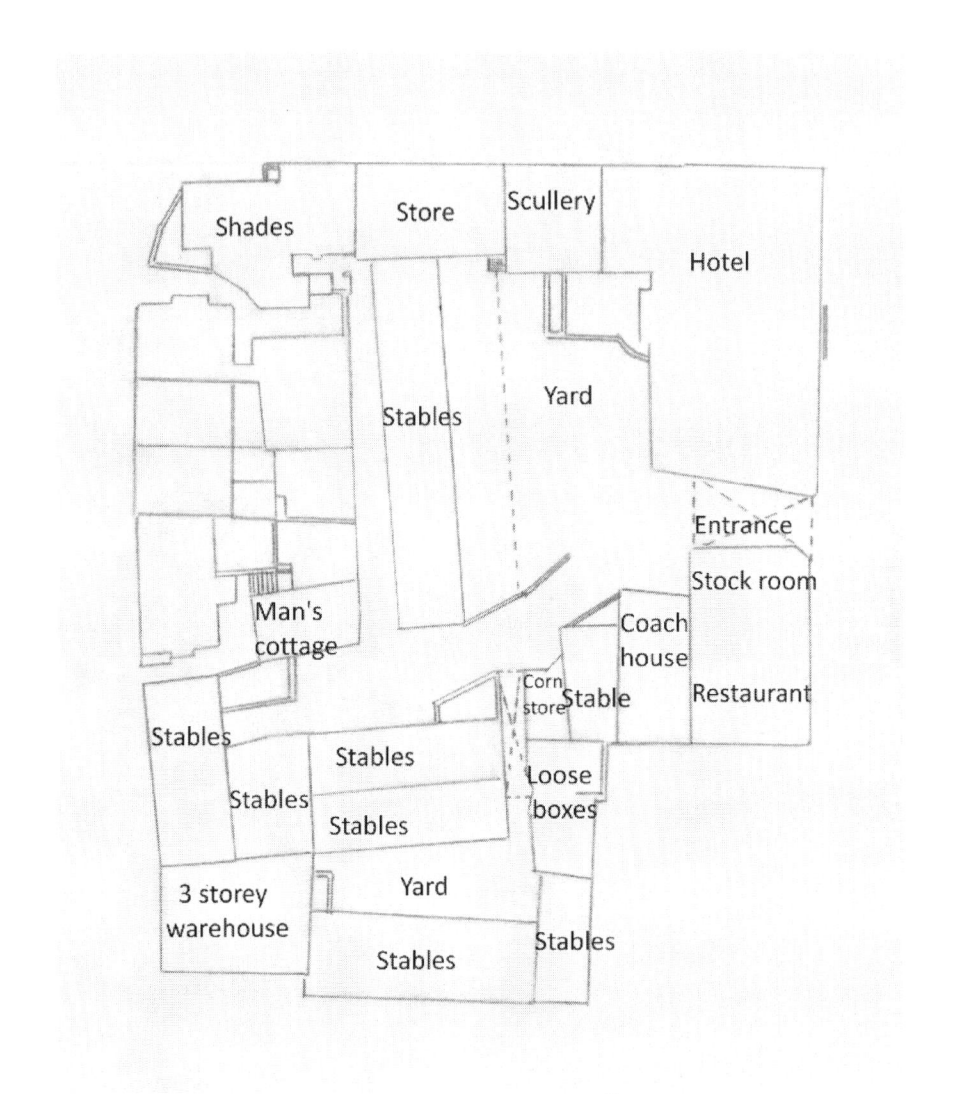

Ground plan 1885–1888 [47]

In May 1888 Joseph Bullman was forced to extend his mortgage by £4,500. He died in the same year and his widow Rosetta Bullman took over for a few months until she was 'released' of her obligations under the lease.[48]

The Swan was put on the market again for a second time in nine months, and in February 1889 was purchased by William and Henry Ellis, Wine and Spirit Merchants of 36 Leadenhall Street, London for £9,000. The higher price presumably included the freehold. They immediately sold it on to local builders John and William Taylor with the aim of rapid redevelopment.[49] The Taylor brothers contracted James Breeds, Auctioneers, to sell off the contents of the hotel and stables, and in the ignominious and shameful end of the old Swan its quality contents, furnishings, horses and carriages were disposed of in what amounted to a flea market in the Swan yard.

By August 1889 the Swan and its estate had been largely demolished and the rebuilding of a new public house, three shops in the High Street and at least 14 houses was mostly completed by January 1890. But in the process the Taylor brothers overreached their financial capacity and vastly increased their borrowing. At least seven further loans were made to them in that year.[50] In 1890 they leased the new public house back to the Ellis brothers for 40 years at a rent of £300 per annum, and sold off some of the new houses and shops. Four and five Swan Terrace, for example, were sold for £1,070, and numbers one to six Swan Avenue were let at nine shillings [45p] per week.[51]

In 1889 the *Observer* reported that 'it is amongst the clergy and churchwardens of the Hastings Rural Deanery that the hotel will be missed, for there were spread the luncheons that followed the visits of the Archdeacon of Lewes in the adjoining church of St Clements'.[52] During the demolition old cast iron fireplaces were found hidden in the walls. They were attached to ornamental firebacks cast at a Sussex foundry perhaps 250 years before. The fireback design however, did not include the image of a swan but of another bird; the phoenix from classical mythology. However, the swan was often depicted with wings expanded argent, which might have looked like a phoenix to the eye of an untrained reporter.[53]

The new Swan was licensed in 1890 after a demand made by St Clements Church that 'the bar in Swan Terrace be kept closed for the whole of Sunday' was agreed. This condition remained in force until the Swan came to the end of its life in 1943. However, the Swan Shades was not re-licensed and in 1889 closed its doors to the public for the last time.[54] It was renamed Silchester House and became a private residence.

Three years later in 1893, the Taylor brothers were declared bankrupt after borrowing and spending £12,940 on the redevelopment of the Swan and its estate. This may not however, have been the final figure. The *Hastings News* reported that they suffered a loss of £2,000, but there is a large discrepancy between information in the legal documents and the report in the local press.[55]

Apart from leasing the new Swan the Ellis Brothers also occupied an adjoining shop and part of the old cellar network. For a few years in the 1890s this part of their business was referred to as Ellis Bros: Swan Wine Vaults. The Ellis Bros were a company of wine merchants long established in the City of London and locally. In Hastings they owned at least two other wine vaults known as: Ellis Bros and Vidlers Ltd, located in Grand Parade, St Leonards and in the Pelham Arcade, Hastings.

The new public house continued under the name of: Swan, London Distillery Company. The London Distillery Company was a division of Ellis Bros formed to run at least three public houses in

Three young boys looking up at the Swan Hotel

SWAN

Hastings, which they acquired between 1887 and 1890. These were the Swan, the York in the town centre and the Warriors Gate, St Leonards.

Although the London Distillery Company were the new owners of these pubs, they were not brewers and the brewery which supplied them is unknown. The London Distillery Company continued operating the Swan until sometime around the start of the First World War. It is not listed in the street directory after 1913. The Swan eventually became tied to Leney's Brewery of Wateringbury, Kent, and later still to Whitbreads.

The opening of the new Swan in 1890 brought much needed improvement to the area. Not only was the old Swan complex completely renewed when all its buildings were replaced by new housing, but the new Swan was set back by six feet [1.82m], allowing the High Street to be widened. This was made possible because of a planning agreement between Hastings Council and the Taylor brothers. The Council obtained the land for free but changed the planning permission to allow the new Swan to be built 10 feet [3.05m] higher than at first granted.[56]

However, the temperance lobby campaigned for the closure of licensed premises, and opposed any application for the renewal of a licence. The *Hastings Advertiser* commented:

> The London Distillery Company recently purchased the Swan Hotel, and have since resold it to Messrs. Taylor Bros. We do not know whether this will disturb the peace of mind of the temperance party in the town, but, at all events, it would seem to suggest that large companies do not share the apprehension that the time is close at hand when publican's property will be seriously interfered with by the Legislature. Recently, as has been pointed out more than once, the sums paid for licensed premises here have been very large, and, in some cases, wholly disproportionate, as many considered, to the value of the property.

Hastings & St Leonards Advertiser 21.03.1889

SWAN

Swan Hotel from the south just before demolition

SWAN

CHAPTER THIRTEEN

FROM INN TO PUBLIC HOUSE

The new Swan

The transition of the Swan from an inn to ordinary public house reflected the social and economic changes that had taken place in the Old Town prior to the Swan's demolition. The Old Town had now become a predominately poor area and the demise of the Swan as an inn was an inevitable break with the past.

The old Swan 'parlors', Assembly Room, high class restaurant and smoking rooms were now only a faint glimmer in the community memory and from now on the Swan was a working-class public house. Nevertheless the redevelopment of the Swan and its estate was a vast improvement to the lower end of the High Street.

The new Swan was described as 'a commodious building whose appearance is superior to most other houses in the High Street'. Its design was synonymous with the latest in Victorian pub architecture which came into vogue in the late 19th century. The large bar, based on the design of the shop counter, was designed for swift service and was ideal for housing the beer engines, ornate

SWAN

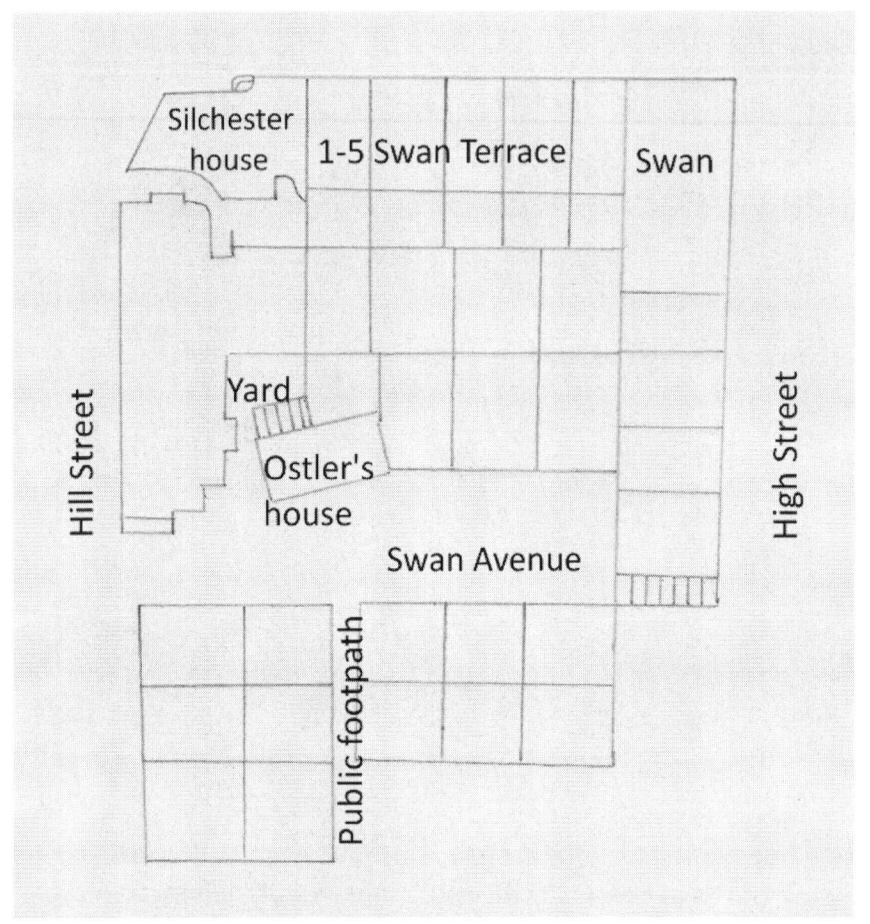

Ground Plan 1890 [57]

mirrors, etched glass, gas lighting, painted tiles, marbling and graining associated with the style. Another feature was that although it provided seating, it encouraged customers to stand at the bar. The new Swan had a saloon bar and two public bars, one with an entrance in Swan Terrace.

An indenture of 1890 between the Taylor brothers and the Ellis brothers included a long covenant which required the Ellis brothers to insure and maintain all the marbling, graining and other modern features of the the new Swan.[58]

During the First World War the competition was extremely tough. Government restrictions and the imposition of the Defence of the Realm Act (DORA) applied especially to towns like Hastings

SWAN

LONDON DISTILLERY COMPANY

ALL ARTICLES ARE OF THE

HIGHEST STRENGTH

AND PUREST QUALITY

SUPPLIED IN SMALL QUANTITIES AT

WHOLESALE PRICES.

	Pkt.	Bot.	Gall
OLD TOM (Booth's)	1/6	1/11	11/6
UNSWTD. GIN (Booth's 22u.p)	1/6	1/11	11/6
RUM (Jamaica)	1/7	2/1	13/-
WHISKY (Irish or Scotch)	1/10½	2/6	14/6
HOLLANDS (De Kuyper's)	1/10½	2/6	14/6
BRANDY (Cognac)	2/-	2/6	15/-
BRANDY (Otards' Old)	2/6	3/2	19/-

SPECIALITIES.

WHISKY Choice Old Scotch or Irish	2/8	3/-	18/-
RARE OLD Ten years in bond	2/8	3/6	21/-
BRANDY (Hennessy's Old)	3/3	4/6	26/-
" (Finest Old Liqueur)	4/-	5/6	36/-

WINES FROM THE WOOD.

3d., 5d., 7d., per quartern.
PORT & SHERRY   1/-, 1/6, 2/3, per pint.
7/6, 12/6, 13/-, per gallon

BOTTLED WINES.

PORTS & SHERRIES,   from 1/- to 6/6 per bottle.
CLARETS,   from 1/- to 6/-   "

See special Bottled Wine List for particulars.

CHAMPAGNE OF ALL BRANDS
At Lowest Shipping Prices.

WE CHALLENGE COMPARISON

SWAN

High Street, 1930s

High Street 2013

where military forces were assembled. By order of the local military authority, Lieutenant-General C. Woolacomb, pub opening hours were reduced by two-thirds and all licensed premises had to close at 9 pm. Beer was watered down, the 'long pull', or the over measure of beer, was banned and it was forbidden to buy anyone a drink under the 'no treating' orders.

At this time, neat spirits were supplied to public houses at a high strength and publicans were required to break down spirits with water. The legal maximum dilution of spirits was 25 degrees under proof, which at times led to problems. The Swan used the pure water from the pump in George Street (now Ye Olde Pump House). In 1919 several licensees were charged with selling spirits under strength and/or at the wrong price or measure. Nellie Venning, landlady of the Swan, was summonsed for selling whisky under strength and overpriced, and was fined £11.2s 6d. [£11.12] after a Food and Drink Inspector walked in and asked for 'a drop of whisky'.

Surprisingly during the course of the 1920s depression there was an increase in the number of licensed premises in the area. By 1929 there were 12 public houses within 200 yards [183m] of the Swan and 26 public houses within 400 yards [366m], demonstrating the excess and density of licensed premises in the Old Town and the culture of the public house which permeated this part of Hastings.

In that year the chief constable opposed the renewal of the Swan's licence on the grounds of redundancy and stated that the Swan was no longer required. He pointed out that there had been nine landlords since 1917 indicating the Swan's poor trade during the depression, and that the rent had been reduced from £200 to £50 a year. The last two landlords confirmed they had suffered losses of £1,000 and £544 respectively. 'This house is not a business proposition', they said. One of the few witnesses to speak up for the Swan was the Reverend H. Cole, Rector of St Clements Church.

Ex-landlord Albert Jones, gave evidence against the brewery, whom he had previously taken to court for 'alleged fraud and misrepresentation'. He had paid £1,167 for the tenancy of the Swan 'as a strong and viable business venture' in 1929 but had only 'got out' £697, making a loss of £470. He also claimed that the five previous licensees had suffered a collective loss of £4,800 between them since 1924. He won his case and was awarded losses against the brewery. This information reinforced the chief constable's opinion that the Swan was no longer needed. Consequently the licence was not renewed.[59]

However, Albert Jones admitted under questioning that as a 'brother Mason' he had lied in a letter to a prospective licensee claiming that the Swan was a profitable business. This was probably under pressure from the brewery.

The 12 pubs within 200 yards of the Swan were:-

> The Mitre, High Street,
> Jenny Lind, High Street,
> Duke of Wellington, High Street,
> Duke of Cornwall, Post Office Passage,
> Hastings Arms, George Street,
> Queen Adelaide, West Street,
> Jolly Fisherman, East Parade,
> The London Trader, East Parade,
> Royal Standard, East Beach Street,
> Lord Nelson, East Bourne Street,
> Kicking Donkey, Hill Street,
> Hole in the Wall, Hill Street.

In 1931 the Swan was reprieved when the licence held by Herbert Cole, of the Mitre on the opposite side of High Street, was transferred to William Dulcie, landlord of the Swan, which reopened in April of that year and the Mitre closed down instead.[60] The Mitre, however, regained its licence some years later as the Mitre Restaurant and more recently as Porter's Wine Bar.

It has been suggested that the landlord of the Mitre requested that his licence be transferred to the Swan. But the question as to why it was transferred remains unanswered. A clue lies in the testimony of Albert Jones who implied that freemasonry was rife in the brewery and among the magistrates, and that this was a major factor in the decision. However, the late Ron Fellows whose father was one of the licensing magistrates said 'my father would not have anything to do with the Freemasons'.

SWAN

The Mitre opposite the Swan 1920–1923

SWAN

The Mitre as Porters Wine Bar 2013

SWAN

CHAPTER FOURTEEN

SWAN IN THE SECOND WORLD WAR

Following the recession of the 1930s, war once more raised its ugly head in September 1939. After the Battle of Britain in 1940 at least 33 public houses closed temporarily due to wartime conditions, depressed trade and stress. Several other pubs including the Bedford, the Denmark, the Norman and the Star in the West, along with much other property, suffered from bombing and air raids.

The Swan however, managed to stay open until May 1943 when it was completely obliterated during one of the worst air raids on the town during the Second World War. The *Hastings Observer* reported that: 'The attack was made by ten fighter bombers which, swooping out of low hanging clouds, crossed the coast at the eastern end of the town, and diving to roof-top height, dropped high-explosive bombs.'[61]

As the Swan collapsed around its terrified customers and staff, falling masonry, the blast and splinters, killed or injured several people drinking and working in the bars. Eleven Swan customers and two staff lost their lives in the attack, along with two children aged three and six.

SWAN

Margaret Hayward at home in 1 Swan Terrace was also killed making a total of 16 casualties.[62] Her son Henry Hayward died in the Swan. Her other son Bill had decided to visit the London Trader instead of the Swan that Sunday lunchtime but returned to find his mother and brother dead. 'I was in the London Trader', he said, 'when suddenly we heard the chatter of machine-gun fire and a couple of bullets came through the window followed by some enormous explosions. We walked up the High Street with dread as people left their houses to look at the damage'.[63]

Another customer who died was life-boatman William Hilder, engineer on the Hastings lifeboat. He had been a crew member on the lifeboat when it went to Dover prior to the Dunkirk evacuation. He had been awarded the RNLI (Royal National Lifeboat Institution) bronze medal but his life was cut short and he never received it.[64]

It is a local belief that the bomb came in from the east and removed the upper storeys of Aylwards Builders Merchants, opposite the Swan, before destroying the Swan itself. The photograph on page 91 shows this not to have been the case, with Aylwards more or less intact. The builders' merchants must have been demolished at a later date.

From 1935 the licence of the Swan was held by the Gummerson family.[65] By 1940 the men of the family were not resident having gone off to war, and the licence was then held by Grace Gummerson, assisted by her sister Hilda. Tragically, Grace and

SWAN

Hilda and Grace's three-year-old son Trevor were among those to lose their lives. Rescue crews worked throughout the night and the following day but found only one survivor and a dog still alive.

The rescue team afterwards expressed their gratitude to the landlord and landlady of another High Street pub, believed to be the Duke of Wellington, for providing them with a continuous supply of refreshment.

A month later in July, Leney's brewery applied to erect wooden shacks as a temporary home for the Swan and the Warrior's Gate in St Leonards, which was also bombed, but this was refused.[66] The

SWAN

official reason given by Hastings Borough Council was that to allow wooden shacks would affect post-war town planning.[67] Although this was no doubt correct a more poignant reason was that the town was still suffering from shock, and this was an insensitive and badly timed application. Consequently the Swan was never rebuilt.

The wartime tragedy of the Swan's destruction and the accompanying loss of life was almost unspeakable, and the town could hardly come to terms with its grief. To avoid further agony the clerk to the Hastings Petty Sessions referred obliquely and indirectly to the devastation when he stated that 'the premises had been rendered unfit for use by an unavoidable calamity'.[68]

The Swan's licence was held 'in suspense' by Walter Daish of Leney's Brewery until 1946, when it was transferred to the landlord of a new pub in Hollington called the Wishing Tree.[69] Thus, along with the licence, the spirit of the Swan returned to its ancestral home in Hollington, the home of its first landlord John Levet.

It has also been claimed that a pair of ghosts, which had haunted the Swan for centuries, accompanied the licence to the Wishing Tree and continued their paranormal activity in that pub. But that, as they say, is another story!

SWAN

Seven years later in 1953 Hastings Borough Council purchased the Swan bomb site for £575 from Leney's Brewery.[70] In a final blow to the Swan a covenant attached to the Land Registry search stipulated that in future 'neither the land ... nor any buildings thereon shall be used for the purpose of sale ... manufacture, storage or advertisement of alcoholic or spirituous liquors, nor any club or other licensed premises in which intoxicating liquors shall be sold or distributed' be allowed.[71]

A notice lodged with the Land Registry in 1952 pointed out that the land was subject to a floating charge, a form of security for capital raised by the brewery. This floating charge was originally created by a deed of 1896 but obviously did not apply to the Swan estate until much later. Whether it still applies is unknown.[72]

Hastings Borough Council also purchased the bomb sites of numbers one, two and three Swan Terrace for £90 each from their private owners. These purchases were made under the 1875 Public

SWAN

Health Act, which allowed the Council to create a small remembrance garden. Today the Swan Memorial Garden is a permanent reminder of this Second World War carnage in the High Street and of 420 years of local history.

Searching for survivors

SWAN

CHAPTER FIFTEEN

FROM SWAN TO WISHING TREE

The application to Hastings Magistrates Court for the transfer of the licence of the Swan to the Wishing Tree was reported in the *Hastings & St Leonards Observer* of 29th June 1946 as follows:-

Bombed Hotel's Licence Moved

FROM "SWAN" TO "WISHING TREE"

One of the worst of the many air attacks in Hastings during the war was recalled at the Magistrates Court on Tuesday, when Mr. F. Miskin (Messrs Bracher, Son and Miskin, Maidstone), on behalf of the licencee Mr Walter George Daish, applied for a "Special removal" of the licence of the Swan Hotel, High-Street, to Nortons, Wishing Tree-Road, St Leonards. The new premises to be known as the Wishing Tree.

Mr Miskin said that on May 23 1943 the Swan premises were completely destroyed by enemy bombs, and unfortunately there was considerable loss of life. The tenant, who had been the licencee, and had gone to the war, was the only survivor. His wife who had held the licence, the whole of their family and a number of other people lost their lives. To-day the premises were represented by a hole in the ground and there was no structure left.

He said that Mr. Daish on whose behalf he was making the application, was secretary of Messrs Frederick Leney & Sons, Pheonix Brewery, Wateringbury, who were the owners of the Swan and also the premises at Nortons, which they recently acquired.

THE NEW SIGN

At Nortons there were five rooms on the ground floor, of which three and a central hall would be given over to public use. The new premises would be named the Wishing Tree instead of the Swan.

SWAN

"The old Swan has had its last song." said Mr. Miskin, "and it is thought appropriate the premises in Wishing Tree-Road should be named the Wishing Tree. By your action in granting this application it is hoped that you will wish it the best of luck in its new destination."

Mr. Miskin produced a picture of the sign which would hang outside the new premises, and said it depicted a wishing tree, at the foot of which was a maiden on the verge of womanhood and underneath the famous advice of Mr Punch to those about to marry — "Don't."

Mr. John Marchant, managing director of Messrs Leney & Sons, gave formal evidence of the destruction of the Swan, and added the rateable value was £48.

Mr. Walter George Daish made formal application for the special removal.

Superintendent Knell said that the police offered no objection, and there being no other objections, the Chairman (Alderman A.W. Chesterfield) said that the application would be granted.

In about 1947, only four years after the bombing of the Swan, Whitbreads published the following anonymous article in their House Journal.

The Swan, The Curse and The Wishing Tree

In this scientific age many of us are inclined to turn up our noses at the idea of a witch's spell. We call it a run of bad luck when a whole string of personal matters go wrong, but are easily persuaded that such a thing is quite impossible with a building or a particular project.

Far be it from brewers, of all people, to quarrel with scientists, to whom they owe so much, but even the most sceptical must hesitate a little before the record of the Swan Hotel at Hastings.

In the days when Hastings was a fishing village nestling under the cliffs, there was an inn on this spot, hard by the Parish Church. Local tradition is that an enraged mother in Cromwell's day placed a curse on the house, when an alleged traitor informed on her son there, and that either two or three successive inns were burned down.

Despite its reputation, the house was rebuilt and by the early 1800s had become the principal posting-house in the town. Later, however, the curse — if curse there be — returned to The Swan, this time in the shape of the railway train, which noisily asserted its presence, and temporarily the hotel was in eclipse.

Builders and brewers were ever optimists, and, trying to forget the past, a new Swan was busily playing its part before Victoria had ceased to reign, but many still living can vouch for a seeming run of misfortune there, some of which can no doubt be easily explained away.

Consider, nevertheless, the Swan's record since it became a member of the Whitbread group but a few years ago. It suffered badly from fire on two occasions. It was closed for a period, and then — almost unique in licensing — was reopened in place of two other houses. It was the scene of a suicide and at least one non-fatal accident. We suffered what seemed a crowning misfortune in 1939, when a very old servant and friend was fatally injured by a barrel which slipped and fell upon him while delivering there.

Yet even worse was still to come, for in May 1943, the house received a direct hit. The Swan was completely destroyed, and all the occupants killed, including many customers as well as the licensee and entire family. The witch's curse had indeed persisted!

Little doubt, then, that even sceptics and cynics sighed with relief when, the war over, it was arranged to remove the licence to another growing part of Hastings at Hollington, there to be known to future generations as The Wishing Tree. Suitable premises were obtained and a minimum of conversion was necessary to make a house worthy of the company.

As a local newspaper man was good enough to write— 'Remembering The Swan's history, nothing could be more apt than the sign of its successor'.[73]

The Wishing Tree

SWAN

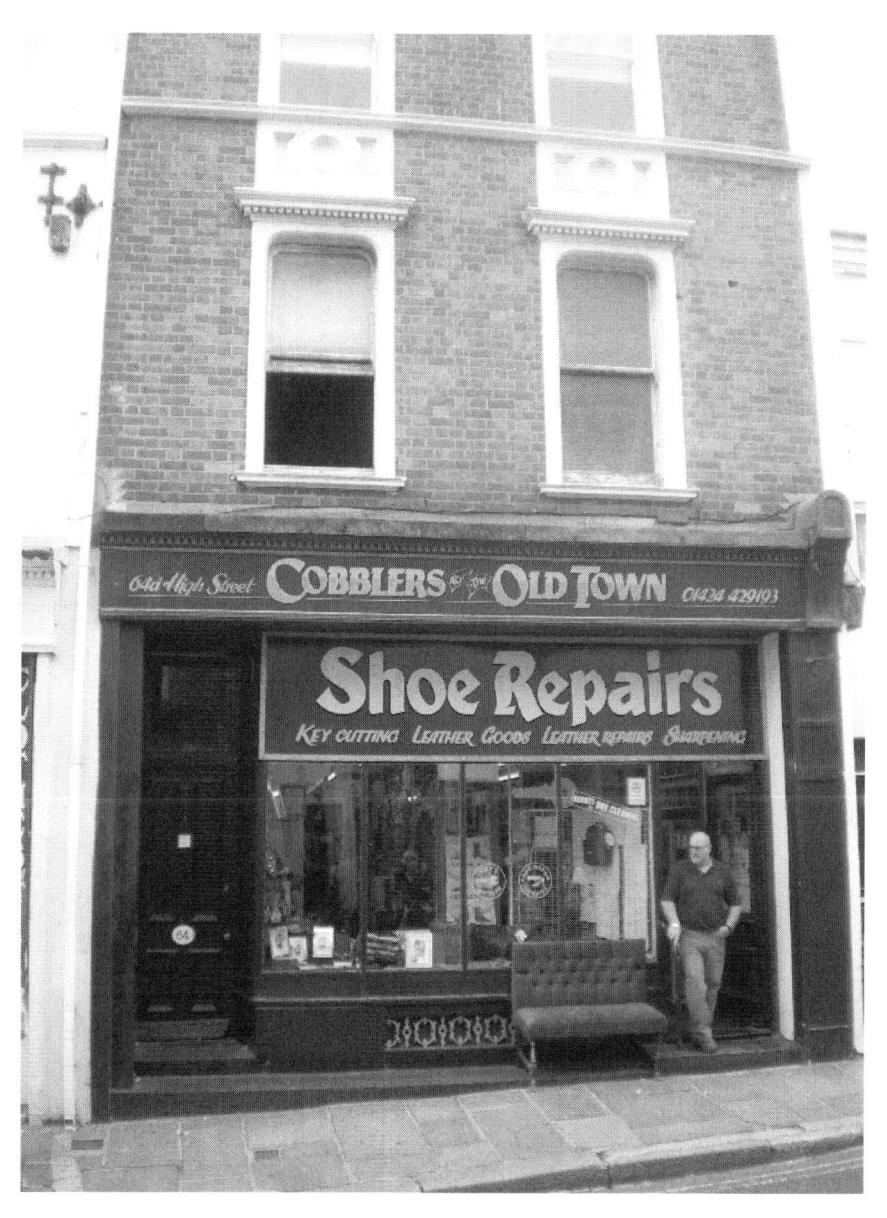

Cobblers to the Old Town, 2013 built on the site of the Swan gateway

SWAN

The corner of High Street and Swan Terrace, 1880s

SWAN

The corner of High Street and Swan Terrace, 2013

SWAN

Swan House Bed & Breakfast in Hill Street, 2013

SWAN

REFERENCE NOTES

The following abbreviations have been used in the references:

HRFHS	Hastings & Rother Family History Society
HSLA	*Hastings & St Leonards Advertiser*
HSLC	*Hastings & St Leonards Chronicle*
HSLN	*Hastings & St Leonards News*
HSLO	*Hastings & St Leonards Observer*
ILN	*Illustrated London News*
NA	National Archive
SE	*Sussex Express*
SWA	*Sussex Weekly Advertiser*

1	Brett *Hastings Premier Cinque Port, Vol 1*, p87
2	Cousins p159
3	Manwaring-Baines 1985 p266-7
4	Harper p10-11
5	Lillywhite p535
6	british-history.ac.uk
7	Clarke p41
8	HSLO 23.03.1889
9	Manwaring-Baines 1968 p4
10	Brett op cit p115
11	Manwaring-Baines 1985
12	Manwaring-Baines loc cit
13	Cousins op cit p285
14	Barry 1797 p69
15	Powell 1817 p22
16	SWA 25.06.1827
17	HSLN 12.05.1848
18	NA SAY 2690
19	Sayer p502
20	SWA 29.04.1771
21	SWA 17.08.1772
22	SWA 15.02.1759
23	SWA 25.06.1827

SWAN

24	SWA/1781
25	Branch-Johnson p120
26	Byng p120
27	Hook p230-4
28	ILN 16.04.1850
29	HSLC 01.11.1854
30	NA DH/B/99/1
31	NA PAR/367/32
32	NA DH/B/83/482
33	NA TAM 14/1/4/4
34	NA DH/B/182/636
35	NA DH/B /83/482
36	NA loc cit
37	NA TAM 14/1/4/4
38	hastingspubhistory.com
39	HSLC 30.08.1865
40	HSLN 02.01.1857
41	HSLO 30.10.1872
42	Manwaring-Baines loc cit
43	HSLC 09.05.1888
44	Correspondence with the author 2.12.2013
45	NA TAM 14/1/4/4
46	HSLC 07.03.1888
47	NA TAM 14/1/4/4
48	NA DH/B/83/482
49	NA loc cit
50	NA loc cit
51	NA loc cit
52	HSLO 23.03.1989
53	Lillywhite loc cit
54	Russell 2011 p108
55	HSLN 02.06.1893
56	HSLA 08.08.1889
57	NA TAM 14/1/4/4
58	NA TAM 14/1/4/4
59	HSLO 08.03.1930
60	HSLO 13.02.1932,12.03.1932
61	HSLO 29.05.1943
62	HRFHS

63	Thornton 1987 p68
64	Thornton loc cit
65	Russell 2011 p106-7
66	NA DH/C/6/2/553
67	HSLO 03.07.1943
68	NA PTS 12/10/7
69	HSLO 29.06.1946
70	NA DH/D/83/482
71	NA TAM14/1/4/4
72	NA loc cit
73	Harper loc cit

SWAN

BIBLIOGRAPHY

Hastings Directories: 1852–1939
Census Returns: 1841–1881
Parliamentary Papers: Select Committee on Public Houses 1852-1853

Books:
Barry, J. (1797) *The Hastings Guide.* Hastings: Barry.
Branch-Johnson, W. (1931) *Wolves of the Channel 1681–1856.*
Byng, J. (1954) *The Torrington Diaries:* Eyre & Spottiswood.
Clarke, P. (1983) *The English Alehouse: A Social History 1200–1830.* Longman Inc.
Cousins, H. (1920) *Hastings of Bygone Days and the Present.* Hastings: FJ Parsons.
Green, K. (Ed)(2010) *Visions of Hastings.* Hastings: Earlyworks Press.
Harper, D. (2005) *Whitbread —The Inn Behind the Signs and a History of the Breweries.* Kent: Harper.
Hastings & Rother Family History Society, (nd) *Civilian War Dead in Hastings, Battle, Bexhill, Rye and Rother Regions (1939–1945).*
Hook, T. (1836) *Jack Bragg.*
Hyde, A. (2004) *The Breeds of Hastings: Merchants and Brewers. 1762–1931.* Brewery History Society.
Lillywhite, B. (1972) *London Signs.* London: George Allen & Unwin.
Manwaring-Baines, J. (1968) *Alehouse and Inn Keepers in Hastings 1595–1836.* Hastings: Hastings Museum.
Manwaring-Baines, J. (1986) *Historic Hastings.* St Leonards on Sea: Cinque Port Press Ltd.
Powell, P. (1817) *Twenty-six Views of Picturesque Scenery of Hastings.* Hastings: Powell.
Russell, D. (2011) *The Pubs of Hastings and St Leonards 1800–2000.* St Leonards-on-Sea: L Russell.
Russell, D. (2013) *Register of Licensees for Hastings and St Leonards 1500–2000.* St Leonards-on-Sea: L Russell.
Sayer,C. (Ed)(1907) *Correspondence of John Collier and his Family 1716–1780.*
Thornton, D. (1987) *Hastings: A Living History.* Hastings: Hastings Publishing.

SWAN

Newspapers:
Hastings and St Leonards Advertiser 1866–1918
Hastings and St Leonards Chronicle 1846–1905
Hastings and St Leonards Gazette 1856–1896
Hastings and St Leonards News 1848–1876
Hastings and St Leonards Observer 1866–1943
Illustrated London News, April 1850
Sussex Express 1837–1943
Sussex Weekly Advertiser 1759–1827

Volumes
Brett, T. *Manuscript History. Volumes 1–7*. Hastings Reference Library.
Brett, T. *Hastings Historico Biographies*. Hastings Reference Library.
Brett, T. *Hastings Premier Cinque Port*. Hastings Reference Library.
Brett, T. *Rhymed Reminiscences of Hastings & St Leonards*.

Website: hastingspubhistory.com
Russell. D. (2010) *Shades Bars on the South Coast*.
Russell, D. (2010) *Hastings Temperance Lobby, 1840–1942*.

A NOTE ON SOURCES

For the general historical setting of the town I have used *Historic Hastings* by John Manwaring-Baines and the manuscript volumes of Thomas Brandon Brett. The latter I have used with caution verifying the 'facts' from other sources wherever possible. All quoted verses are taken from Bretts *Rhymed Reminiscences of Hastings and St Leonards.*

The bulk of this history however, has been constructed from a pot pourri of primary sources. Local newspapers in conjunction with local guides and directories, have as usual yielded much information. Much more however has come from the National Archive both online and at East Sussex Record Office, Lewes.

The National Archive is the location for the ground plans of the Swan complex and for the plan of the Assembly Room drawn in 1880. Due to the fragility of the original documents they cannot be photocopied. For this reason they have been redrawn by Lynda Russell. They are not exactly to scale but are nevertheless reasonably accurate.

The National Archive is also the location of several deeds, mortgages, petty sessions registers, covenants and other documents relating to the Swan and these are referenced accordingly.

When quoting people from the 18th century I have maintained their original style of expression. This includes, for example, the contemporary spelling of certain words and the overuse of capital letters etc. which was then the custom.

APPENDIX 1

Casualty list of the 1943 Air Raid on the Swan

1. Violet Cox, 32, killed by the collapse of the building.
2. Grace Gummerson, Landlady, 31, killed by the blast.
3. Hilda Gummerson, 32, killed by falling masonry.
4. Trevor Gummerson, 3, killed by falling masonry.
5. William Hart, 47, killed by the blast.
6. Henry Hayward, 43, killed by falling masonry and the blast.
7. William Hilder, 56, killed by falling masonry.
8. Joseph Pepper, 62, killed by the blast.
9. James Phillips, 46, killed by the blast and splinters.
10. William Reed, 46, killed by falling masonry.
11. William Roffe, 85, killed by the blast.
12. John Somerville, 48, killed by the blast.
13. Ann Tester, 6, killed by the collapse of the building.
14. George White, 78, killed by the blast and falling masonry.
15. Thomas Winborn, 55, killed by the blast.
16. Margaret Hayward, 79, killed by falling masonry at 1 Swan Terrace.

Source: Hastings & Rother Family History Society: *Civilian War Dead in Hastings, Battle, Bexhill, Rye and Rother Regions. (1939–1945).*

SWAN

APPENDIX 2
Register of Licensees

Swan Hotel, High Street

1523	John Levet
1600	James and Elizabeth Lasher
1604	John Homan
1604–1606	Anthony Wennell
1634–1636	Francis Wennell
16??	Mrs Hay
1642–1652	Robert Marshall
1685	Richard Watts
1685–1693	Thomas Gawin
1696–1716	Margaret Gawin
1716–1717	Mercy Gawin
1722	Katherine Stevens
17??	Richardson family
1726–1729	Mrs Grove
1730–1740	Richard Halstead
1729–1747	Mercy Halstead (widow)
1742–1750	William Gurr
1751	Widow Gurr
1751–1770	Thomas Breeds
1758	John Collier (owner)
1760	Mary Collier (owner)
?	Henrietta Collier (owner)
?	General James Murray (owner)
1771–1776	Thomas Hovenden
1776–1799	William Scrivens
1800–1801	Jeremiah Wicken (owner or freeholder)
1802–1811	Thomas Stockwell "
1812	Thomas Breeds (2) "
1799–1815	James Dodson
1820	Edward Wenham
1816–1824	Charles Mott

SWAN

1825–1835	Francis Emary & Abraham Wood
1836–1839	William Eldridge
1839	George Robinson
1841–1864	William Carswell
1865–1873	Elizabeth Carswell
1874–1884	Joseph Collins
1885	John Plowman
1886	Mary Plowman
1887	Joseph Bullman
1888	Rosetta Bullman
1889	Charles Bullman
1889	Henry Stanbury
1890	Harry Sidney
1891	John Cook
1892	George Goutage
1892	Charles Moore
1892	George Hutchison
1893	William Dennington
1893	Frederick Attenborough
1894–1896	Frederick Russell
1897	Albert Rix
1898	William Lowe(ry)
1899	Thomas Ronald
1900–1902	William Glass
1902	Ernest Crane
1903–1917	George Vening
1918–1922	Nellie Vening
1922–1923	Charles Tidey
1923	Henry Gill
1924–1926	William Moorecroft
1927	Harold Heath
1928	Whiting Osgerly
1928	Isobel Osgerly
1929	Albert Jones
1929–1930	William Dulcie
1930	(Licence cancelled)
1932	(Licence transferred from the Mitre)
1932–1935	Albert Tooth

SWAN

1935–1940	Ernest Gummerson
1940	Kate, Hilda & John Gummerson
1941–1943	Grace Gummerson
1943	(Bombed. Licence held in suspension by Walter Daish)
1946	(Licence transferred to the Wishing Tree)

Swan Shades, Swan Terrace

1800	Edward Humphrey
18??	Thomas Martin
1826	John Hazleden
1828	John Golding
1839	Charles Winter
1840	Mr Farrol
1845	Joseph Norman
1853	Frank Winter
1860	John Friend
1861	Rosina Willett
1862	William Willett
1867–1868	Louis Griffin
1872	Charles Griffin
1878–1883	Thomas Henham
1884–1888	Stephen Blundell
1889–1890	Charles & William Taylor
1890	(Closed)

Sources: Hastings Petty Sessions Registers, National Archive and Hastings newspapers.

APPENDIX 3

'A Schedule of Tenants' Fixtures at the Swan Hotel' 1886

All the stoves as fitted in the several rooms throughout.
All the bells, cranks, wires as fitted in the several rooms throughout.
The Iron Gun Barrel and other piping as laid to the gas burners in the several rooms throughout.
Painted numbers on all doors, all finger plates and trade lettering throughout.

Second Floor:-

Mahogany shelving on the landing and a brass bolt on the WC.

First Floor:-

Work fitted to outside window to form a fernery.
Ball Room: Handsome marble chimney piece, 2 raised deal platforms, speaking tube fitted to the bar, embossed glass panels in doors, mahogany wood work. Seven well modelled figures 5 feet high as fixed on brackets.
Store and Closet: mahogany desk and pigeon holes.
Lavatory by billiard room with Jennings patient urinal, marble basins with brass taps.

Ground Floor:-

Bar Parlour: 3 feet mahogany cupboard and shelf.
Commercial Room: Moulded hat rail as fixed 28' run. Boots bell and engraved brass plate, gilt moulding around the room. Two 2 feet ceiling ornaments to gasoliers.
Entrance Hall and passage: Dwarf gate at the bottom of the stairs to the ball and billiard room.

SWAN

Lobby: 11 feet and 18 feet runs of shelving.
Bar: Painted and grained oak counter with pewter top and fittings, 4 feet by 3 feet mahogany plate cupboard, marble slabs in larder, mahogany letter box.
Store and closet adjoining Coffee Room: for crockery.
Kitchen: 8 feet Kitchener with ovens, hot plates 4 feet by 2 feet in brickwork, gas stove 4 feet by 2 feet in brickwork.
Erection of tin hot chamber with range.
Wash House: 32" copper in brickwork. 30" iron pan, service pipe and tap. Pot hooks in the chimney. Plate rack.
Cook's Pantry: Cupboards and shelving etc

Yard:-

Meat safe, 4 feet by two feet by two feet, bottle racks.
No 1 Cellar: Cheese store.
No 2 Cellar: Brickwork forming wine bins.
No 3 Cellar: Brickwork forming wine bins.
Stables, Loose Boxes and stalls. Two paddocks. Office 'under yard', Desk with flap.
Chicken house.
Pheasant house.
Ostler's cottage: 3 feet, 6 inches range in kitchen. Old stove and copper in scullery. Stove in bedroom.

External:-

Ornamental lamp over entrance.
Lettering 'Swan Hotel' on the front and east side of the house.
Lamp at side entrance. Ostler's bell.

Source: National Archive.

APPENDIX 4

Oil Paintings of William Francotte 1883

Hastings Museum and Art Gallery has in its collection, a pair of oil paintings by William Francotte presumed to be a resident of Hastings in the late 19th century. The paintings which are dated 1883, are of the Swan Inn and the Swan Shades and were acquired by the museum in 1952. The painting of the Swan Shades is the only pictorial representation of that building that has come to light so far. There are no known photographs.

A second pair of oil paintings unsigned and undated but obviously copies of Francotte have surfaced. The copies are exact except for some deliberate changes of detail. In both the Francotte paintings an anonymous figure of a man in an apron poses outside both buildings. In the copies he is missing from the Swan Shades but is accompanied by a second figure in a bowler hat outside the Swan. Some other details have also been changed.

On closer examination of the copies some advertising on the wall of the Shades is that of Leney's Brewery, of Wateringbury, Kent. There is some historical anomaly here as the Swan was not tied to Leney's Brewery until around the time of the First World War, some 30 years after 1883. Also the Shades became a private house in 1890.

Thus the advertising must have been added in at some point between 1913 and 1952. Nothing is known about William Francotte and these two paintings seem to be his only known work. He remains a shadowy figure from the 19th century.

SWAN

Anonymous copy of William Francotte's oil painting of the Swan

SWAN

Anonymous copy of William Francotte's oil painting of the Swan Shades

SWAN

Swan Memorial Plaque